DATE DUE

Courts and Public Policy

Courts and Public Policy

CHRISTOPHER E. SMITH

The University of Akron

NELSON-HALL PUBLISHERS
Chicago

Project Editor: Rachel Schick
Cover: *Sulfanilamide*. Sulfanilamide is an organic chemical photographed here through a miscroscope (with crossed polarizing filter) and shown at fifty times magnification. Photography by Joseph Barabe for McCrone Associates, Westmont, IL.

Library of Congress Cataloging-in-Publication Data

Smith, Christopher E.
    Courts and public policy / Christopher E. Smith.
    p. cm.
    Includes bibliographical references.
    ISBN 0-8304-1294-8
    1. Courts—United States. 2. Judicial process—United States.
3. Judicial power—United States. 4. Public policy (Law)—United
States. I. Title.
KF8719.S55   1993
347.73'1—dc20
[347.3071]   92-38092

Manufactured in the United States of America

10 9 8 7 6 5 4 3 2 1

FOR ALICIA AND ERIC

CONTENTS

vii

CONTENTS

PREFACE

Debates about the appropriate role of the judicial branch have raged for several decades. As judicial decisions have shaped the contours of public policy concerning a variety of issues, commentators have argued about whether judges have exceeded their proper authority under the United States Constitution and whether the impact of contemporary courts upon American society has been beneficial or detrimental. Many of the arguments about judicial intervention into policy issues are grounded in normative constitutional theory. Other conclusions about courts and public policy flow from case studies of judges' actions in particular cases or on particular policy issues. Because there are both normative and empirical questions underlying debates about judicial policy-making, neither of these approaches by themselves adequately capture the complex processes that comprise policy-shaping actions in the judicial branch. Principled philosophical arguments and individual case studies readily produce conclusions about judicial policy-making. The quest for definitive judgments may, however, impede recognition of the less visible judicial attributes that provide the basis for broader understanding of courts' limited power and questionable effectiveness within the policy-producing interactions and processes of the American political system.

This book represents an effort to synthesize scholars' arguments and findings about judicial policy-making. The chapters that follow will discuss the normative questions about the proper scope of judicial authority under the constitutional governing system as well as the practical questions about courts' policy-making capabilities. Individual chapters will discuss judicial intervention into specific policy issues as a means to illuminate the complex, political nature of the judicial policy process. A chapter on the cumulative impact of civil litigation will demonstrate how judicial processes affect American society in ways that extend beyond traditional characterizations and debates about judges as deliberate policymakers.

Because analyses of judicial policy-making inevitably involve evaluative judgments that negate any assertions of "objectivity" by commentators, this book makes no special claims about an absence of bias. As in any other book, and because of the subject matter, perhaps more so than in many books, the author's evaluative judgments are evident. However, because this book's primary purpose is to illuminate the complex political interactions within the judicial policy process rather than to reach a definitive judgment about the value, legitimacy, or desirability of judicial policy-making, the author's discernible viewpoints should not interfere with any reader's desire to make judgments about this book's controversial and important subject matter. If the book fulfills its intended purpose, it will not prevent the development of judgments, either pro or con, about judicial policy-making. Instead, it will provide sufficient "food for thought" so that readers who harbor preexisting conclusions about judicial policy-making will critically reexamine those conclusions and readers who subsequently reach conclusions about courts and public policy will make considered judgments that reach beyond ideological reflex and overgeneralizations based on single-issue analyses.

My knowledge about and analysis of judicial policy-making have been influenced by several people. I am eternally indebted to my mentor and friend, George Cole of the University of Connecticut, for giving me my initial exposure to this subject. Although he does not fully realize it, my discussions with Harry Stumpf of the University of New Mexico gave me greater insights about the influence of politics in the judicial process. I have also benefitted from my continuing association with my former student and sometime co-author, Scott Johnson of the Ohio State University. In addition, I am grateful to the hundreds of students who have taken my courses on the Supreme Court, judicial process, and public policy at the University of Connecticut's Hartford campus and at the University of Akron. They have pushed me to develop the questions and insights that provided the basis for this book.

I am indebted to other people for encouraging and facilitating the completion of this book. My colleagues in the Political Science Department at the University of Akron have provided a congenial and supportive environment for inquiry, research, and writing. Mari Bell

Nolan and Bonnie Ralston provided their usual superb assistance with the preparation of the manuscript. In addition, Richard Meade and the others at Nelson-Hall deserve a special "thank you" for their continued support of my project ideas.

I am most indebted to my family for support and patience as I wrote this book during a particularly hectic year. My wife, Charlotte, rearranged her law school studies and probably sacrificed some of her own academic achievement to permit me to spend hours in front of my personal computer. The book could not have been completed in a timely manner without her efforts and understanding. I am dedicating this book to my children, Alicia and Eric, who provided pleasant diversions from the demands of writing and who, in my mind's eye, represent the next generation of policymakers who must learn from the experiences of preceding generations in marshalling the resources of government to confront society's pressing social problems.

CHAPTER 1
COURTS AND PUBLIC POLICY

IF INDIVIDUAL HUMAN BEINGS LIVED
alone and isolated from other people, there would be little reason to
have rules for behavior and mechanisms for distributing benefits and
burdens. Obviously, conflicts over land, property, and other matters
can occur only when there is someone with whom to dispute. When
people come into contact with other people and live in communities or
societies, the maintenance of order and social stability requires that
people follow established rules and procedures in order to avoid
chaos and conflict. Societal rules may come from customs or religious
beliefs developed within a particular culture. The rules may also come
from an authoritative figure or organization that possesses both the
legitimacy and social acceptance necessary for public acquiescence to
decisions and the power to force compliance with decisions. In some
societies, the rule-making and norm-enforcing figures may be religious leaders, military commanders, or hereditary rulers. In other
societies, responsibility for authoritative decisions is vested in structured organizations, namely governments. The placement of decision-making authority in government not only facilitates the creation
and enforcement of rules, it also creates a mechanism for defining,
seeking, and hopefully achieving collective goals intended to benefit
the entire society. In American society, these authoritative decisions
on behalf of society are what we think of as *public policy*. Scholars have
debated the appropriate definition for the term "public policy." The
simplest definition states that "[p]ublic policy is whatever governments choose to do or not do."[1] Decisions and actions by government

1

establish rules (e.g., at what age may someone legally purchase an alcoholic beverage) and allocate benefits and burdens (e.g., how much shall each citizen pay in taxes and how will government revenues be spent). This simple definition of public policy recognizes that society is affected not only by the actions taken by government but also by governmental inaction.[2] For example, because the federal government has declined to emulate European countries' national health care plans, more than thirty-four million Americans lack insurance coverage to pay for medical expenses.[3] Thus the distribution of medical services is shaped by government inaction.

There is no consensus on a definition for the term "public policy" because there are disagreements about whether the definition should merely include governmental decisions (and non-decisions) and their social consequences or whether discussions of public policy must necessarily include the entire *process of policy-making*, including agenda setting, decision making, policy implementation, and policy consequences.[4] In order to avoid the pattern evident in other books in which authors assert their own flawed definitions for public policy after criticizing several definitions offered by other writers,[5] the chapters that follow will eschew precise definition and take a broad approach by examining processes, decisions, political reactions, and outcomes from the courts' involvement with authoritative decisions that affect American society.

Courts And Policy-Making Within the American System

Within a democratic governing system, public policy decisions are especially important because contending politicians, political parties, and interest groups compete with each other in an effort to gain control of or influence over authoritative decision making. These political actors seek to advance their values and self-interest through the implementation of their preferred public policies. Because the American courts have had a significant impact upon many policy issues (e.g., education, abortion, criminal justice, etc.), commentators scrutinize and debate the appropriateness and effectiveness of the judicial branch's influence over public policy. As judges actively involve themselves in the formulation and implementation of policy decisions, critics warn that the judicial branch will (or has) become too politicized: "[Judicial] nominees will be treated like political candidates, campaigns will be waged in public, lobbying of senators and the media will be intense, the nominee will be questioned about how he [*sic*] will vote, and he will be pressed to make campaign promises. . . ."[6] Thus, fears that judges will behave just like partisan politicians in legislatures or in the executive branch are part of the debate about the judicial branch's proper role (or lack thereof) in policy-making. Although debates rage about the propriety and extent of courts' impact upon public policy, critics and supporters of judicial policy-making agree that courts have exerted a powerful influence over the shape of American public policy.

Judges are clearly involved in policy-making through "the establishment and application of authoritative rules."[7] Their actions influence what government will do or not do concerning certain policy issues. Judges do not merely create abstract rules to guide behavior. Judicial decisions directly affect people's lives in many ways. An individual court case may decide no more than who owes money to whom in a dispute between two individuals. Judicial policy-making may be present even in such seemingly small cases because a governmental entity, namely the judiciary, is utilizing its official authority and power to allocate resources within society and to influence the development of rules affecting future allocative decisions. By contrast, other court cases are more easily recognizable as affecting public policy. Judicial decisions may, for example, determine whether a state government needs to spend millions of dollars on a new prison or whether women have a right to obtain abortions. As one of the three branches of government, the judiciary provides a forum in which people can seek to advance their goals for directing governmental actions and for allocating societal resources. Groups and individuals who lack the political power to influence the policy-making decisions of legislatures and executive branch officials may present their policy objectives as legal claims in order to seek assistance from judges.

Because decisions by the U.S. Supreme Court affect the entire country, discussions of judicial policy-making frequently focus upon the nation's highest court. However, other courts within the judicial system influence the development of public policies, too. State trial courts provide the initial forums for cases that will help set the policy agenda for a state or even for the country. In state trial court cases, arguments are developed, political interests are mobilized, and baseline judicial policy decisions are made that provide the basis for subsequent reviews, if any, by appellate courts.[8] United States district courts, the federal system's trial courts, similarly provide the initial forums for many policy issues. Federal district judges have developed and implemented many of the most controversial judicial policy decisions affecting the administration of school systems, prisons, and other institutions.[9] State appellate courts influence public policy development for many different issues.[10] For example, even though the U.S. Supreme Court has declared that the U.S. Constitution permits Congress and state legislatures to forbid the use of public funds for poor women's abortions, the Michigan Court of Appeals decided in 1991 that Michigan's state constitution provides broader abortion rights, including access to state funding, than those contained in the national constitution.[11] Because the U.S. courts of appeals are the final decision makers for many federal cases, their role as policy-making entities "has continued to grow."[12] Although the processes that underlie the development of decisions differ within each of these levels of the American court system, all of these courts face fundamental questions about the legitimacy and capacity of judges for developing effective public policies.

Policy-Making Authority

The authors of the Constitution of the United States met in Philadelphia in 1787 to design a system of government for the young nation. Based upon their beliefs in such ideas as representative democracy and the avoidance of the excessive accumulation of power in any single entity, they created a governing system composed of separated national legislative, executive, and judicial branches. They also reserved many powers for individual state governments and, eventually, provided for the protection of individuals' rights by adding the Bill of Rights to the Constitution in 1791. It is evident from the specific provisions within the document that the Constitution's framers expected the legislative branch to bear responsibility for creating public policy, namely the behavioral rules, governmental programs, and other actions that would advance the collective interests of the nation's citizens. Thus Congress was granted the authority to regulate interstate commerce, to declare war on behalf of the country, to "define and punish Piracies and Felonies committed on the high Seas," and to undertake various other decisions that are regarded as *policy-making*.[13] Because of the democratic ideal of citizen control over government through the electoral process, the framers placed primary decision-making authority in the hands of the governmental branch that was most representative of the country's diverse regions and that was most susceptible to control by voters' decisions in frequent elections.

As a relatively brief document that was written in 1787 and that contains many general provisions, the Constitution could not specifically anticipate and provide answers for all of the problems that would confront the United States over the course of two centuries. The framers of the Constitution could never have anticipated the processes of technological advancement, immigration, industrialization, urbanization, and other elements that challenged governmental decision makers to develop new policies to advance the citizens' collective interests in stability, peace, and prosperity. As the nature and complexity of problems changed, so too did the distribution of decision-making authority. The original assumptions about congressional primacy over policy decisions diminished as the other branches of government asserted themselves in response to new kinds of problems. For example, although the Constitution gives the multi-member Congress the power to declare war on behalf of the country,[14] can the United States wait for 535 legislators to meet, debate, and vote on such a decision in a nuclear age in which attacking missiles may reach the country in less than one hour? Obviously, the country needs to respond immediately to such situations. Because major decisions in the single-headed executive branch can be made quickly, the necessities of modern warfare contributed to an expansion of presidential authority over decisions about military affairs. Although the example of nuclear weapons presents the starkest case of the need for executive power, as the nation's constitutional "Commander[s]-in-Chief,"[15] presidents actually began to assert their authority over such matters much earlier in American history. Abraham Lincoln, for example, ordered a blockade of southern ports during the Civil War before Congress had acted to declare war.[16]

Although the changing nature and complexity of problems facing American society contributed to the altered distribution of policy-making power, social developments were not the sole or primary cause of such changes. The distribution of authoritative decision-making power also changed because, under the general provisions of the Constitution, there are opportunities for strategic maneuvers by the political actors within each branch of government who seek, through assertions of authority, to enhance their respective branches' recognized constitutional powers. For example, although the specific provisions of the Constitution merely authorize the president to make treaties (with the advice and consent of the Senate) and appoint ambassadors, presidents have asserted much broader authority over foreign affairs.[17] Members of Congress have occasionally challenged the president's authority on such matters, but the president has consistently succeeded in maintaining a dominant role in formulating the country's foreign policy.

Judicial influence over policy-making developed through judges' successful assertions of authoritative decisions concerning policy issues. Although the authority to do so is not stated in the words of the Constitution, the federal judiciary gained the power to review and to invalidate acts of the other branches of government

5

through the assertion of such authority in 1803[18] and the exercise of such authority in subsequent decades.[19] As judges increasingly came to view themselves as the guardians of the people's civil rights and liberties, judicial decisions began to shape public policy explicitly. During the late nineteenth century and early twentieth century, for example, political conservatives on the Supreme Court protected the interests of businesses by invalidating governmental efforts to regulate the economy and initiate social welfare programs.[20] From the 1950s through the 1980s, political liberals in the federal judiciary invalidated governmental practices that fostered racial discrimination,[21] inhibited free speech,[22] and subjected criminal defendants and prisoners to unduly harsh treatment.[23] The conservative judges' actions in the earlier era were based upon the protections for economic rights that they perceived to be contained within the Constitution; the liberal judges' subsequent actions were premised on their view that the Constitution embodies ideals of human dignity for all individuals. Thus the ambiguity in the Constitution's words provided the opportunity for judicial officers from both ends of the ideological spectrum to assert their authority and shape public policy.

Judges and the Debate about Judicial Policy-Making

Despite the ample evidence that courts are political institutions whose composition, decisions, and effectiveness are shaped by the actions of partisan political interests, judges are often reluctant to insert themselves forthrightly into debates about the judiciary's role in politics and policy-making. For many judges, this reluctance may stem from firmly held views about proper judicial roles, self-delusion about the nature and extent of courts' impact upon society, or calculated strategies to protect the judiciary's public image. Because obedience to judicial authority is presumed to rest upon the courts' image and legitimacy as non-political institutions and neutral decision-making forums, judges may be hesitant to evaluate and discuss judicial involvement in politics and policy-making.

For example, in judges' characterizations of themselves and their role within the governing system, they do not share a consensus concerning whether they are, in fact, policymakers. Judges have faced this question directly in several legal cases in which laws creating mandatory retirement ages for state judges have been challenged as violative of the federal Age Discrimination in Employment Act. Under the Act, only workers on "the policymaking level" may be forced to retire when they reach a specified age. If judges acknowledge that they are policymakers, then the mandatory retirement provisions can be applied to judicial officers. If, however, judges do not regard judicial officers as policymakers, then the application of mandatory retirement provisions to judges would violate the federal law. A federal circuit court in Missouri upheld the regulations by acknowledging that "whatever the philosophy of the particular judge, and whether he views his proper role as broad or narrow, his decisions—some of them, at least—necessarily will resolve issues previously unsettled and thus will create law."[24] By contrast, a federal circuit court in New York ruled that such regulations do not apply to judges by asserting that "[t]he performance of traditional judicial functions is not policymaking. . . . The principal business of the courts is the resolution of disputes."[25] Although these decisions reflect traditional divisions in judges' and commentators' portrayals of the judicial role, it is clear from examining the substance and consequences of judicial decisions that judges can and do have notable effects upon public policy. In fact, although the U.S. Supreme Court ultimately tiptoed around the issue of whether or not judges are policymakers, the justices upheld the application of the retirement law to state judges by conceding that judges exercise their discretion on issues of public importance and therefore can be regarded as "on the policymaking level."[26]

Concerns about maintaining the courts' image as "legal" rather than "political" institutions affect both the public's perceptions about the nature of the judicial branch and the legal community's presentations to the public about the court system.[27] The subtitle of Robert Bork's best-selling book, *The Tempting of America*, is "The Political Seduction of Law."[28] This subtitle captures and reinforces the commonly-held view that courts are supposed to be neutral governmental decision-making forums that are insulated from the partisan political influences that are so open and pervasive in the other institutions of government. This view naively ignores and therefore finds objectionable the reality that politics necessarily determines the content of law and the decisions of courts. Political processes determine which individuals will don the black robes of judicial officers, either through presidential appointment and Senate confirmation in the federal system or through elections and gubernatorial appointments in state systems.[29] Judges bring to the bench their accumulated knowledge and experience as well as inescapable attitudes, values, and policy preferences. Indeed, Chief Justice William Rehnquist concedes that "[t]he law is at best an inexact science. . . . There simply is no demonstrably 'right' answer to the question involved in many of [the Supreme Court's] difficult cases."[30] Judges, who are products of partisan struggles within the political system, must create "the law" through their value-laden judgments. Judicial decisions are also shaped by the strat-

7

egies and reactions of interest groups, legislatures, and other political actors who initiate cases, hinder the implementation of judicial policies, or otherwise fight against judges' decisions with which they disagree. Because courts are political institutions, the process of judicial policy-making is inevitably affected by the strategies and tactics of interested political actors.

Stages in the Judicial Policy-Making Process: Agenda Setting and Decision Making

The chapters that follow will discuss the development and consequences of judicial decisions affecting various illustrative policy issues. Although the actions of interested individuals and organizations differ within each issue area, there are common elements to the judicial policy-making process that affect most policy issues. Most notably, the courts' agenda must be set by the initiation of legal actions in forms that are processable by the courts and at moments when judges are receptive to such issues. Thus interest groups and individual lawyers are frequently influential actors in the judicial policy process. Any analysis of the role of courts in policy-making requires a basic understanding of judicial processes and the important actors who influence those processes.

Courts provide a forum for airing disputes between individuals, groups, and organizations. In civil cases, one party requests a judicial declaration concerning the respective rights of the disputants to property, compensation for an injury, performance of a contract, or some other asserted entitlement. Commentators often divide civil cases into two general categories, disputes limited to two private parties and lawsuits aimed at generating social change. Since the 1950s, many interest groups have utilized litigation to pursue their public policy agendas through the courts. Civil lawsuits have contributed to the desegregation of school systems, the improvement of conditions within prisons and jails, the opportunity for women to make choices about abortions, and many other policy outcomes. Scholars have noted, however, that it is not always easy to distinguish between private disputes and social reform litigation. Sometimes a case may begin as a private dispute and subsequently become transformed by the lawyers or judges into something bigger.[31]

Interest Group Litigation

Typically, reform-seeking litigation involves a lawsuit against a governmental agency by an individual, often backed by an interest group,

8

seeking judicial protection of an asserted constitutional right. Private individuals and interest groups may also explicitly pursue social change through suits against other private entities. The Southern Poverty Law Center, for example, has filed suits against the Ku Klux Klan and other white supremacists. Although these actions ostensibly seek monetary compensation for racially-motivated murders of innocent African-Americans, the Center is quite frank about its underlying goal of eliminating racist organizations by destroying them financially and thereby deterring other such organizations from engaging in violence and intimidation.[32] In the late 1980s, corporations began to utilize civil litigation against individual community activists who opposed the development of landfills, incinerators, and other pollution-causing business projects. The corporations file multimillion-dollar defamation suits claiming that their citizen-opponents hurt their business by making false statements. Few defamation lawsuits aimed at individual activists succeed in court, but many such suits achieve their intended purpose by scaring the individual citizens away from opposing corporate plans because of the litigation costs required to fight such suits and the fear of losing money after a trial.[33] Thus, civil litigation does not exclusively advance the interests of political underdogs. Litigation is a tool available to any interests that have legal resources and access to the courts.[34] Litigation is simply the form of "lobbying" that political interests can employ in order to influence government and public policy through actions by the judicial branch.

Studies of liberal groups generated the commonly-held view that interest groups that successfully employ litigation strategies are typically political underdogs. These groups sought to advance their policy goals in the judicial branch because they lacked the necessary access and resources to influence public policy developments successfully in the legislative and executive branches. For example, as chapter 4 will discuss in greater detail, advocates of equality for African-Americans had little ability to influence legislatures during most of the twentieth century. A variety of devices (e.g., poll taxes, complex registration requirements) were employed in many states to prevent African-Americans from voting. Thus they had little ability to influence the decisions of elected officials. In addition, they lacked the organizational and financial support necessary for effective lobbying campaigns. In order to seek the elimination of laws and practices that fostered racial discrimination in housing, education, and voting, civil rights groups sought judicial assistance.[35] The courts were virtually the only forum within government that provided an opportunity for African-Americans to present their claims for full citizenship rights during most of the twentieth century. Civil rights lawyers, especially those from the National Association for the Advancement of Colored People (NAACP), scored significant legal victories in court cases that helped to enhance equal opportunity and to end official racial discrimination by government. The success of civil rights groups' attorneys on behalf of African-Americans provided a model for interest group litigation by advocates for women, prisoners, the disabled, environmental issues, and other causes.

Although politically liberal groups became associated with the strategy of litigation, politically conservative groups increasingly used litigation as a means to achieve their policy goals or to fight against the policy achievements of their liberal political opponents. Conservative groups employed litigation strategies early in the twentieth century to oppose unions, government regulation of business, and other developments in society with which they disagreed.[36] After witnessing the success of liberal interest group litigators in the 1950s, 1960s, and 1970s, a variety of conservative groups created their own legal organizations devoted to the pursuit and protection of their favorite policy issues in the courts. The increased litigation activities by these organizations during the Reagan era, in which they had sympathetic allies in other branches of government, indicates that interest groups no longer pursue litigation because they have no other government forums available to hear their claims. Instead, as Lee Epstein's studies indicate, "a wide range of groups regularly resort to the judicial arena because they view the courts as just another political battlefield."[37]

In order to employ litigation strategies successfully, interest groups need several attributes and resources.[38] Interest groups need sufficient longevity to pursue the frequently incremental process of pursuing judicial decisions that shape a particular public policy issue. It required several decades of continuous litigation in dozens of cases before the NAACP finally persuaded the Supreme Court to rule against racial segregation in public schools. Organizations need financial resources and adequate staff, both legal and clerical, to maintain litigation, especially when challenging more affluent interests or government—entities that can afford to prolong the litigation process. A group's ability to generate well-timed publicity enhances its ability to litigate policy issues. Positive publicity can generate financial support and favorable public opinion as well as provide broader circulation of the legal arguments and evidence that the group wishes the judiciary to consider. Publicity in the form of law review articles can educate the legal community, including judges, about the soundness of arguments advanced by an interest group. Groups benefit from respectability in the eyes of the judges and the public. A group's reputation may affect its ability to attract the support of other interest groups for a litigation campaign. For example, if an avowedly racist organization wishes to pursue a case concerning government limitations on its members' ability to give public speeches, other organizations concerned about free speech issues may shy away from any association with a group known for espousing despicable ideas.

Litigation Strategies

One primary strategy employed by interest groups is the sponsorship of test cases. When organizations sponsor test cases, they may represent a claimant whose case raises issues in a desirable fashion. Sponsorship of test cases can require significant commitments of time and money because it may take several years for a case to work its way through multiple levels of the state and federal courts. Sometimes organizations will become sponsors after a case has presented a specific policy issue to a trial court. In such cases, the organizations' attorneys may be more skilled in the preparation and presentation of appellate arguments than the litigant's original attorney.

From the interest group's perspective, sponsorship of cases permits the group to exert control over the arguments presented to courts concerning specific policy issues. In other words, the individual claimant's case serves as the vehicle for the presentation of the political interest's views in the judicial arena. For example, when the officers of the Executive Committee of the Southern Cotton Manufacturers Association sought to fight the implementation of federal laws that limited the working hours of child laborers, they strategically planned the type of case and specific court that they would use to challenge federal legislative authority to create labor laws. Within the jurisdiction of the sympathetic judge whose court they had selected as the forum for initiating the case, they toured factories to search for desirable claimants to provide the vehicle for a legal challenge to national public policy. Instead of formally representing the group's members, namely the factory owners whose labor forces would be affected by child labor laws, they found a family of textile workers who were willing to serve as plaintiffs. Thus the issue could be presented to the judiciary as the case of a working-class family seeking the freedom to permit their children to continue earning income rather than as a case of business interests challenging unwanted government regulations.[39] Because the carefully planned case fit neatly with the predisposition of that era's Supreme Court justices for preventing government from regulating economic activities, the Southern Cotton Manufacturers Association won a significant (albeit temporary) legal victory on behalf of businesses.[40]

Not all interest groups can successfully "plan" their legislative initiatives. As Stephen Wasby's research on the NAACP's civil rights litigation campaigns indicates, interest groups' litigation activities are shaped by a variety of internal and external factors.[41] For example, interest groups must shape their arguments within the limitations of the particular issues raised by the cases of the claimants who present themselves to the group for assistance. A "perfect" case may not be available for presenting the desired issues to the courts in the most beneficial fashion. Organizations' governing boards and central office staff members may disagree with attorneys about the criteria for selecting cases and the strategies for presenting cases in court. Attorneys must react to the litigation strategies of their opponents and to the interim decisions made by judges (e.g., whether certain evidence is admissible, etc.). Thus attorneys cannot readily control the pace or direction of litigation within specific cases.

An alternative interest group litigation strategy is the submission of *amicus curiae* briefs to appellate courts. These "friend of the court" briefs are written arguments filed with the court in support of one particular party in a case in which the interest group is not a direct participant. Initially, *amicus* briefs were used to provide judges with useful information from a neutral third party outside of the litigation. Gradually such briefs came to be used to support one party's position in a particular case. The use of *amicus* briefs has grown to such an extent that they are now a standard element in cases heard by the U. S. Supreme Court. During the 1940s, only 18 percent of cases heard by the Supreme Court included *amicus* briefs. By 1988, 80 percent of cases included *amicus* briefs.[42]

The *amicus* brief may present an opportunity for the interest group to provide the judges with additional arguments in support of or in opposition to a policy position. Interest groups may also build coalitions through the use of *amicus* briefs by demonstrating to the judges how many different organizations agree or disagree with a particular policy position. Thus groups will invite other interest groups to submit briefs or to "sign on" to a brief filed by an allied interest group.[43] In some instances, the credibility and expertise of a particular interest group may persuade judges about the desirability of a particular outcome. If a case concerns medical issues, for example, medical arguments presented on behalf of physicians' organizations may provide judges with useful and persuasive information that was not effectively presented in the partisan arguments of the competing parties directly involved in the litigation.

The Role of Lawyers

In order to push disputes along through each stage of civil litigation, people must seek the advice and assistance of lawyers. In effect, lawyers are "gatekeepers" who determine which cases will enter the judicial process and which cases will stop short of the courthouse door. Lawyers play an important role in transforming disputes into legal cases. Lawyers must translate people's disputes into legal terminology in order to pursue them as cases in court. In cases concerning policy issues, lawyers are especially influential because their arguments and evidence provide the basis for judges' decisions. Lawyers play an important role in defining the policy issue for the court, suggesting legal rationales to justify judicial intervention, and recommending potential remedies that judges might order to advance the preferred policy outcome.

Lawyers do not expect to pursue successfully all of their preferred policy initiatives through the judicial process. Previous court cases inform the lawyer that it may be pointless to translate specific disputes into legal cases. For example, if a man wishes to pursue a claim against a police department that refused to hire him because of the length of his hair, the man could be genuinely and legitimately angered from being victimized by a discriminatory criterion that bears little or no relation to his qualifications to become a police officer. Unfortunately for this discrimination victim, a lawyer would have to tell the man that nothing could be accomplished by pursuing the case in court. Civil rights laws only cover specified categories of discrimination (e.g., race, color, national origin, etc.) and courts have already declared that employers can discriminate against men because of the length of their hair.[44] Although lawyers can use creativity to develop arguments linking new kinds of claims to recognized legal concepts, some claims simply do not fit within the contours of contemporary legal principles. Legal concepts are sufficiently malleable that many arguments are plausible. Because judges determine the course of the law within the judicial process, however, the lawyer must consider whether the particular judges who will decide the case will be amenable to new arguments. For example, because the U.S. Supreme Court was dominated by conservative Republicans in 1990, there was little reason for lawyers to pursue new arguments seeking an expansion of rights for criminal defendants. Thus, lawyers may discourage claimants from pursuing certain disputes as legal cases. For many years, people with enough money could pay a lawyer to present almost any argument in court. In the 1980s, however, judges began to assess financial penalties on lawyers and litigants who present frivolous

13

claims, so lawyers have much more reason to discourage clients and to decline to present disputes that do not fit within recognized legal principles or within the realm of new ideas that might be accepted by the individuals who are sitting as judges.[45]

Judicial Decision Making

After interest groups or individuals initiate policy-oriented cases, they await the next stage of the judicial policy process, decision making. Like the other stages in the policy process, judicial decision making is influenced by complex, political factors.

Litigants bring their disputes to courts because they have certain expectations about the nature of judicial decision making. Although they expect judges to issue considered judgments after thorough and fair examinations of all relevant arguments and evidence, litigants in public policy cases are usually keenly aware of the political leanings of the judges before whom they appear. If litigants genuinely believed that judges are wholly biased or unfair, they would not spend the time and money to pursue their claims through the judicial process—unless they believed that the judges' biases would work in their favor. In some instances, lawyers may also believe that an adverse decision will generate favorable reactions from a sympathetic public or otherwise help to lay the groundwork for subsequent favorable policy actions.

Public confidence in the judiciary is maintained through the use of symbols, which help to perpetuate the myth that judicial decision making is neutral and objective. Judges wear black robes and sit on elevated benches, characteristics that separate judicial officers from the citizens who come to them seeking wise and fair judgments. The public must stand in respectful deference as the judge enters and leaves the courtroom. The physical environment of the courtroom, which frequently includes high ceilings, marble columns, wood paneling, or other visible symbols such as the scales of justice, reinforces the judicial branch's image as a serious institution that deserves public respect and obedience. The formal, solemn environment of the court, with its robed decision makers and traditional procedures, is more akin to religious institutions and ceremonies than to any other setting in American society. Moreover, the use of "law" as the purported basis for decision making reinforces the judicial branch's symbolic elements to reassure the public that judges are different from other authoritative decision makers such as legislators and other elected officials, whose decisions are affected by greed, self-aggrandizement, and partisan political interests. The imagery employed to maintain the judiciary's legitimacy is designed to convey the impression that judges are society's learned elders whose special knowledge of law enables them to make neutral and just decisions.

Are judges really neutral, unbiased decision makers whose special knowledge of law provides clear answers to the difficult questions brought to courts for resolution? Of course not. Beneath the black robes are human beings who were placed in their authoritative judicial positions through the operation of the political system. Like other people in American society, judges possess values, attitudes, biases, and political interests that affect their decisions. Judges' knowledge of law provides them with tools to create decisions that will appear proper and legitimate to the public. In some instances, established law may provide examples and principles for a judge to utilize in assessing a dispute. In other cases, legal knowledge merely supplies the techniques for rationalizing and justifying judges' personal preferences so that the public will perceive and accept the judges' decisions as based upon law.

Many lawyers and judges would strenuously object to any characterization of judicial decision making that equates judges' behavior with that of other actors in the political system. They would argue that judges employ established courtroom procedures for the thorough consideration of evidence. Unlike politicians who pursue their own self-interest, judges must follow the precedents established in prior legal cases. Despite the heartfelt sincerity that may underlie such arguments, one should not blindly accept lawyers' and judges' perceptions about the judicial process. They are actors within the system who are socialized through their legal education to accept and defend an idealized image of the judicial system. Moreover, they benefit from the public's deference to and respect for legal institutions. As Harry Stumpf observed, lawyers and judges "can hardly be faulted for packaging and marketing a product that is in such large demand by the public."[46] The public wants to believe that the judiciary is the repository of wisdom and justice. The public wants to believe that there is one governmental institution capable of neutral decision making. If it were otherwise, a loss of public confidence might detract from the courts' dispute-processing and stability-enhancing functions for society. Thus, the judiciary's defenders are merely reinforcing the valuable social functions that derive from the courts' image and legitimacy in the eyes of the public.

How do we know that judicial decision making is influenced by personal characteristics and political factors rather than determined merely by neutral, legal principles? Systematic analyses of judicial decisions reveal the inconsistency and creativity within judicial decision making that are indicative of judges' ability to determine case outcomes without regard for established legal precedents. Moreover, the theories and methodologies of social science have enabled scholars to identify influential factors associated with particular judges' decisions. For example, federal appellate judges tend to make different decisions concerning criminal and civil liberties cases depending upon whether the judges were appointed by Republican or Democratic presidents.[47] Democratic appointees are much more likely to decide cases in favor of criminal defendants and individuals claiming that their rights have been violated. If the outcomes of judicial cases were determined by established principles of law, then there should not be systematic disparities in judicial decisions, such as those existing between judges with different political party affiliations. Political party affiliation is not the sole factor found by social scientists to be associated with particular kinds of judicial decisions. Other studies have shown that judges' prior professional experiences[48] and policy preferences[49] are also associated with particular kinds of decisions. For example, Lawrence Baum asserts that Supreme Court justices follow their attitude-based policy preferences in deciding cases:

> [J]ustices' policy preferences, which can be summarized in ideological terms, are perhaps the most important factor influencing their behavior. . . . [D]ifferences among the justices stem chiefly from their preferences, and the basic direction that most justices take on the Court seems to reflect the attitudes about policy issues that they bring to the Court.[50]

The interpretation of facts and expression of values within judicial decisions are also affected by judges' role orientations. The basic premise of role theory is that individuals act differently within their institutional context than they do when acting in relative isolation. According to a leading theorist, a role consists of "behaviors that are characteristic of persons in a context."[51] Thus, a judge's role is a pattern of behavior that is determined by his or her expectations, the normative expectations that others have for the judge, and other factors that inform the judge's conception of judicial officers' functions in the governing system.[52] In other words, the effect of judges' role conceptions is to limit the expression of what judges want to do (i.e., their policy preferences) because the judges also seek to do what they think they *ought to do* according to their beliefs about a judge's proper role and behavior. Sometimes by fulfilling their conception of their judicial role, namely what they believe judges ought to do, judicial officers will decline to advance their actual policy preferences within a case decision. In James Gibson's words, "the basic function of decisional role orientations is to specify which variables can legitimately be allowed to influence decision-making, and in the case of conflict, what priorities to assign to different decision-making criteria.[53]

Judges' role orientations have been studied on state supreme courts,[54] state trial courts,[55] federal courts of appeals,[56] and the U.S. Supreme Court.[57] One well-known study examined the U.S. courts of appeals and found that federal appellate judges viewed themselves as "Innovators," "Realists," or "Interpreters."[58] Innovators felt that they were obligated to make new law and to influence public policies whenever a case presented them with the opportunity to do so. These judges did not view their judicial role as limiting their ability to express their policy preferences, but instead believed that judges should seek to "launch[] new ideas."[59] Interpreters, by contrast, believed that judges should have a limited role in merely interpreting the law in the context of specific cases.[60] Therefore, these judges restrained the expression of their policy preferences in order to prevent case decisions from usurping the authority of the legislative and executive branches by broadly influencing public policy. On the U.S. Supreme Court, this kind of role orientation was illustrated by four justices who said that a Texas statute designed to prevent illegal alien children from attending school was "senseless" and "folly," and that they would never adopt such a harsh policy themselves.[61] However, these justices dissented against the majority's decision to declare the statute unconstitutional because they believed that judges should not interfere with educational policy decisions enacted by legislatures.[62] Realists took a middle position in which they were careful to avoid improper influence on public policy. Although these judges were willing to restrain their policy preferences if they felt that a judge's decision on a particular issue should be limited, they would make broad decisions concerning other issues which they felt required judicial action.[63]

Although judges determine case outcomes under the guise of legal decision making, judicial officers are not free to make any decisions that they wish to make. There are numerous constraints, both supplied by the individual decision makers themselves and imposed from the external political environment, which serve to limit and create boundaries for the range of the possible decisions. As Gibson concluded after a thorough review of the social science literature on judicial decision making, 'judges' decisions are a function of what they prefer to do, tempered by what they think they ought to do, but constrained by what they perceive is feasible to do.'[64]

How does the external political environment affect judicial decision making? For example, developments in the political system determine the composition of the judiciary. The composition of the judiciary, in turn, shapes the decisions and outcomes produced by the judicial branch. Although political elites from certain demographic groups (i.e., whites, males, and affluent people) dominate the judiciary, the links between the judicial branch and the political system help judicial decisions reflect changes and trends in American society and thereby provide a mechanism for law to develop in accordance with evolving societal values. When new leaders are elected to offices that influence judicial selection (e.g., president, governor, senator, etc.), these officeholders can fill judicial vacancies with judges whose values and policy preferences coincide with those of the contemporary elected officials. If the preferences of the electorate change, those changes can be reflected in the choice of judicial appointees by the officerholders elected in subsequent elections.

Other Stages in the Judicial Policy Process

As subsequent chapters of this book will discuss in greater detail, the external political environment also affects two later stages in the judicial policy-making process, policy implementation and policy consequences. The implementation of judicial decisions depends upon public acquiescence or the exercise of enforcement powers by other branches of government. Judges cannot easily ensure that their directives are followed properly. Judges also cannot readily anticipate all of the consequences that their policy-shaping decisions may produce. Even when a judicial policy is fully implemented, reactions to judicial decisions by other political actors may help to determine whether the judges' policy intentions are fulfilled. As chapter 3 will discuss, judges' lack of control over the implementation and effectiveness of court decisions is a prime concern of those who criticize judicial policy-making.

Recognizing Complexity

Debates about the appropriateness, extent, and impact of judicial policy-making are often presented in stark "pro and con" terms. Although these debates generally tend to attract antagonists with strongly-held, conflicting political philosophies, even someone who consciously attempted to analyze these issues "objectively" would still face grave difficulties in making unbiased conclusory judgments. No observer can analyze judicial policy-making in an objective, detached manner because conclusions about courts' impact upon society necessarily involve value judgments. The fundamental question usually seems to be whether the governing system and the quality of individuals' lives became better or worse as a result of judicial decisions affecting education, criminal justice, and a variety of other policy issues. Those who view the constitutional framework of the American government as reserving all policy-making power for elected officials make strong arguments against judicial intervention into policy questions. By contrast, those who believe that the Constitution emphasizes judges' responsibility for the protection of individuals' rights see judicial policy-making as necessary, inevitable, and beneficial. In analyzing the effectiveness of judicial policy-making, the respective sides tend to emphasize available arguments and evidence that support their predetermined, philosophically-based viewpoints.

In its effort to shed light on the fundamental debate about the judiciary's role, this book seeks to demonstrate that the complexity of the judicial policy process undercuts simple conclusory arguments that characterize judicial policy-making as "good" or "bad." When the complex, political processes that shape judicial policy-making are properly understood, courts appear to be less powerful and less effective in undertaking policy-making than, respectively, their critics and supporters believe. Because the intimate connection between the courts and the political system make judicial policy-making inevitable in the American constitutional system, it may be most useful for people who study the judicial branch to seek insights about the less visible details of the policy process rather than to aspire to make quick, definitive judgments about a complex, recurring phenomenon.

CHAPTER 2
THE LEGITIMACY OF COURTS AS POLICY-MAKING FORUMS

THE UNITED STATES CONSTITUTION
provides the blueprint for the American governmental system. The
Constitution divides the government into three separate branches
(i.e., legislative, executive, judicial) and describes the powers possessed by each branch. The three branches cannot act as they please
because the United States has a system of "limited government." The
powers of the respective branches of government are limited and
defined by the provisions of the Constitution. Theoretically, if the
Constitution does not empower a branch of government to undertake
a particular action, that governmental branch is not authorized to take
that action. Any actions by a governmental actor that exceed the powers granted to it by the Constitution are improper and illegitimate.
Thus a major question that arises when courts become involved in policy-making is whether such actions are legitimate under the American
governmental system. Do courts have the authority to shape public
policy? In order to assess the propriety and legitimacy of actions taken
by the judicial branch that affect public policy, one must begin by
examining the Constitution.

Judicial Power and the Constitution

The United States Constitution vests "the judicial power of the United
States" in the Supreme Court and other federal courts.[1] As in other

sections of the document, the general language of the Constitution does not provide clear guidance on the extent of judicial power. Does this "judicial power" include the authority to formulate and implement public policy? If one examines the intentions of the Constitution's framers, it can be argued that they did not intend to authorize the judiciary to affect the development of public policy. As described by an important political figure of the founding era, Alexander Hamilton, the judiciary was intended to have limited ability to determine policy outcomes:

> The judiciary . . . has no influence over either the sword or the purse; no direction either of the strength or of the wealth of the society; and can take no active resolution whatever. It may truly be said to have neither FORCE nor WILL, but merely judgment; and must ultimately depend upon the aid of the executive arm for the efficacy of its judgment.[2]

Although this quotation implies that the judiciary will not take an active role in policy making, other words within the same essay indicate that judicial decisions will indeed affect public policy. Hamilton could not have anticipated the magnitude of the twentieth-century judicial involvement in the development and application of governmental policies, but his description of courts' fundamental responsibilities for protecting the Constitution provides the basis for judicial policy-making:

> [T]he courts were designed to be an intermediate body between the people and the legislature, in order, among other things, to keep the latter within the limits assigned to their authority. The interpretation of the laws is the proper and peculiar province of the courts. A constitution is, in fact, and must be regarded by the judges, as a fundamental law. It therefore belongs to them to ascertain its meaning, as well as the meaning of any particular act proceeding from the legislative body.[3]

As the definers and protectors of the Constitution, judges must affect public policy in those instances in which they tell the legislative and executive branches that a particular action cannot be undertaken because that action is unconstitutional. Thus the authority to define and limit the actions undertaken by other branches of government inevitably gives the judiciary power over the shape of public policy. But who will limit and control the judiciary's exercise of power? How do we know that the judiciary will not go too far? These are the central questions in the debate over the legitimacy of judicial policy making.

Constitutional Democracy and the Case Against Judicial Policy-Making

The primary argument against judicial policy-making is that it produces public policy in an undemocratic manner. As designed in the Constitution, American democracy creates mechanisms for the people to determine public policy by electing leaders and holding them accountable for their actions. Presumably, citizens vote for particular people to be members of Congress or the president because they believe those people will do the best job of formulating and implementing policies that will benefit the country. Because the American governing system is a democracy, when the people are dissatisfied with the performance of government officials, they can elect new leaders at the next election. The essence of democracy can be summarized in two concepts: *citizen participation in government* and *accountability*. If these elements are lacking in a governing system, then the citizenry no longer rules its own country. The people are thereby being ruled by a small group of power-wielding leaders.

When assessed in light of these essential elements of democracy, policy-making by courts cannot avoid causing discomfort. In presenting the underlying characteristics of the federal judiciary, the Constitution emphasizes independence rather than accountability. Federal judges are appointed by the president and confirmed by the Senate. They cannot be removed from office by the voters because they serve "during good Behaviour," which effectively means for life. In rare instances, federal judges may be removed through the impeachment process for committing criminal acts or gross ethical improprieties. However, federal judges may not be removed from their positions merely for making unwise, unfair, unpopular, or harmful decisions. Critics of judicial policy-making argue, with good reason, that it is dangerous to permit unaccountable officials to shape public policy. There are strong risks that such officials will impose their own ideas upon the country even though the citizenry desires different policies. In a democracy, the citizens should be the ultimate decision makers concerning public policy, not unelected, life-tenured judges.

In a famous dissenting opinion, Justice John Harlan argued that judicial policy-making leads to a "'mistaken view of the Constitution and the constitutional function of [the judiciary]. . . . [that assumes] every major social ill in this country can find its cure in some constitutional 'principle,' and that [courts] should 'take the lead' in promoting reform when other branches of government fail to act."[4] Members of Congress, many of whom feel that judicial policy-making intrudes upon their authority for developing public policy, have indicated their concern about the impropriety of excessive judicial action. During the confirmation hearings for his Supreme Court nomination, Justice David Souter referred to the occasional need for courts to fill the political vacuum by taking action when elected officials fail to address a social problem. In response to Souter's comment that courts "are forced to take on problems which sometimes might be better addressed by the political branches of government," Souter's Republican supporters on the Senate Judiciary Committee became alarmed and questioned him closely about his views on judicial policy-making.[5] Souter quickly reassured the senators that he did not believe courts should attempt to solve all social problems simply because elected officials have failed to act upon them. If the courts acted to handle all perceived problems not addressed by elected officials, citizen control over public policy and governmental accountability would be greatly diminished.

Not only is judicial policy-making undemocratic in the sense that it lacks citizen participation and accountability, it may actually have corrosive effects upon democracy. If citizens become accustomed to judicial control over public policy, they may no longer debate issues during elections. Similarly, legislators may no longer work to identify and redress social and economic problems that affect the nation. The public may become passive, apathetic, and deferential as it waits for the black-robed guardians of the judiciary to initiate solutions to the country's problems. One of the virtues of democratic self-government is that it keeps the people and their elected officials deeply aware and involved in the major public issues of the day. It forces elected officials to address or avoid the great issues of the day and then subsequently face the voters' judgment for their action or inaction. Elected officials could avoid their responsibilities for governing if the courts handled all of the controversial issues. This would further erode the democratic elements of citizen participation and government accountability. Ultimately, according to Christopher Wolfe, "the loss of political education through self-government . . . may endanger the foundations of a free republic."[6]

American Constitutional Democracy and the Case for Judicial Policy-Making

If one defines democracy as citizen control over government and public policy, the policy-making decisions by federal judges can indeed be considered undemocratic. However, is this really the appropriate conception of democracy under the American constitutional system? American constitutional democracy is not based entirely upon the election of government officials and subsequent elections to hold them accountable. The Constitution also has a Bill of Rights that contains a list of rights for individuals that the government cannot violate. The Bill of Rights serves as the basis for freedom of speech, freedom of religion, the right against self-incrimination, and other familiar protections. It is the responsibility of the courts to insure that these rights are protected. The independence granted to the federal judges through their life tenure permits them to make decisions that clash with popular opinion in order to protect individuals' rights under the Bill of Rights. In making these decisions, judges will inevitably shape public policy because they will be telling elected officials what those officials must or cannot do. Thus, the American constitutional democracy can be defined as citizen control over public policy *plus* the protection of individuals' rights. Under this conception, there is an inevitable role for the courts in keeping the public policy actions of other governmental actors from infringing upon the rights of individuals.

What if the Bill of Rights did not serve as a basis for judicial actions that shape public policy? Without the Bill of Rights, elected officials could respond more freely to the desires of the voters who placed them in office. This would create a very "democratic" environment emphasizing citizen control and governmental accountability, but which citizens would control and which citizens would be adversely affected by governmental policies? Elected officials often follow their perceptions about the preferences expressed by the majority of voters. If public opinion is running strongly for or against a particular policy, it will create pressure upon government officials who wish to retain their positions after the next election. However, public opinion does not necessarily control public policy. The elected branches of government are structured to respond to well-organized and affluent interests. Elected officials respond to wealthy interests that can donate money to political campaigns and thereby advance politicians' personal goal of remaining in office. Politicians also frequently avoid collisions with the preferences of well-organized and well-financed organizations that might mobilize resources against elected officials at the next election. Thus, political action committees, corporations, and other wealthy, well-organized interests exercise significant control over legislative policy making.[7] For example, despite favorable public opinion on gun control, national health insurance, and tax reform, legislative proposals have been thwarted by the opposition of well-organized, well-financed interest groups. There are other examples of interest group influence, such as the close relationships that develop between interest groups concerned with particular policy issues and the executive branch agencies and congressional committees that are supposed to regulate those issues. The historically close relationship between tobacco companies and the U.S. Department of Agriculture, for example, led government officials to fight against health warning labels on cigarette packages.[8]

The policy-making operations of the legislative and executive branches, with their close links to the electoral process, inevitably favor the policy preferences of either electoral majorities or organized political interests. As a result, there are serious risks that the interests of weak political minorities and unorganized or poor groups will be ignored in the policy process. Moreover, the advancement of interests according to public opinion and electoral pressure may create "tyranny of the majority" in which political minorities are actually victimized. The maintenance of racial segregation, for example, advanced the interests of the white majority that gained privileges as African-Americans were excluded from full participation in the economic system and other aspects of American society. For most of American history, racial discrimination was very "democratic" in the sense that it was supported by a majority of citizens and the elected officials that they placed into public office. American history is filled with such "democratic" policies in which the preferences of the electoral majority led to severe discrimination against women, Japanese-Americans, Jehovah's Witnesses, and others groups that lacked sufficient numbers and political power to protect themselves in the electoral process.

Judicial policy-making is not inherently illegitimate when considered in light of the American constitutional system's conception of democracy: citizen control over policy-making *plus* protection of individuals' rights. Judges must identify and enforce limitations upon majority policy preferences when the protected constitutional rights of individuals are threatened by those policies.

Legitimacy as a Complex Issue

The foregoing discussion is not intended to provide a final answer to the difficult question of whether or not judicial policy-making is legitimate for each and every policy issue. Because of the Bill of Rights and federal judges' responsibility for protecting individuals' rights, judicial influence over public policy is not only generally legitimate, it is also inevitable. A recognition of a proper role for courts in public policy does not, however, resolve the troubling questions about judges' actions in shaping public policy. The persistent questions are not the simplistic ones concerning whether judicial actions are legitimate, but rather the more complex ones concerning *which* judicial actions are legitimate. Although judges may properly take some actions that influence public policy, how far can they go in shaping public policy? The issue of prisoners' rights provides a good example of the complexity surrounding the legitimacy issue. If asked about the issue, a majority of Americans would very likely say that prisoners have too many rights and that American society should treat more harshly those people who are convicted of committing criminal offenses. A majority of Americans may even wish to return to an earlier era in American history in which prisoners had no rights and courts regarded convicted criminal offenders as "slave[s]" of the state.[9]

If a majority of Americans believe that prisoners should have no rights, how can it possibly be appropriate for judges to enforce policies that provide protections for these people who have harmed society? The words of the Constitution provide the basis for judges to scrutinize governmental policies that affect prisoners. The Eighth Amendment, for example, forbids the application of "cruel and unusual punishments." These words clearly indicate the existence of limitations upon what the government can do to convicted criminal offenders. The government may punish criminals, but the punishment may not be "cruel and unusual." Because these words are general and ambiguous, there is no easy way to determine which punishments violate constitutional standards. The judges must interpret the Constitution in order to decide whether specific actions by government officials violate the Eighth Amendment. Should judges use these words to interfere with the decisions of governmental officials who supervise correctional institutions? In assessing this question, consider the kinds of questions that have arisen from actions taken by American prison officials: Should someone serving a short prison sentence be permitted to die from injury or disease by being deprived of medical care? Should corrections officials be permitted to use beatings or electric shock torture to kill prisoners who were not sentenced to death? Should a prisoner serving a short sentence be permitted to suffer lifelong physical harm from being malnourished while incarcerated? As these questions imply, there are serious risks that corrections officials might apply "cruel and unusual punishments" if judges cannot shape correctional policies by placing limitations upon the treatment of convicted offenders.

Convicted criminal offenders are a despised political minority who lack the power to influence public policy and who have earned their despised status by causing harm to society. Historically, the American public has evinced little concern about the treatment of convicted offenders. Elected officials have little incentive to prevent the application of "cruel and unusual punishments." Because "the crime problem" is such a popular political issue, elected officials gain their greatest benefits by working to increase the harshness of criminal punishments. As the guardians of the Bill of Rights, judges must define the boundaries of acceptable punishment for convicted offenders. When viewed in this context, it is understandable that judges shape correctional policy by preventing torture and other actions initiated by government officials. The recognition of a role for the courts in shaping public policy does not, however, answer the more difficult question about the breadth of legitimate judicial authority. How far can judges go in identifying rights for prisoners by giving meaning to the words "cruel and unusual punishments"? When do judges go too far?

Although judges may have a legitimate role in limiting the actions of corrections officials, there is also a risk that judges will apply their own personal preferences in identifying rights for prisoners. For example, judges may order expensive renovations at prisons that force state governments to remove government funding from other programs in order to spend more on corrections. Such judicial orders may even force state officials to raise taxes. Decisions about raising and spending governmental revenues have traditionally been regarded as properly under the control of elected officials who can be held accountable by the voters. If a judge orders an expensive new prison to be built, does that have the same effect upon the citizens as "taxation without representation," the very concept that led the American colonists to seek freedom from the British king? The citizens cannot remove the judge from office and they cannot directly change the judge's decision. Thus troubling questions remain concerning the evident risks that judges may exceed the limits of their legitimate judicial authority and thereby interfere with decisions that should be left to the citizenry and its elected representatives in government.

Limitations Upon Judicial Policy-Making

The question of the legitimacy of judicial policy-making cannot accurately be posed as a "yes or no" proposition. The most difficult issues stem from uncertainty about how far judges may go to enforce the Bill of Rights. Although commentators may discuss judicial policy-making as if it is either proper or improper, lurking beneath the discussion are actually disagreements about what poses a greater risk to American society, judicial dictatorship from court involvement in public policy or tyranny of the majority from public policy control by legislative and executive branch officials? Those who seek to curb judicial policy-making believe that judges go too far and thereby damage the American democracy. Defenders of judicial policy-making believe that judges must actively guard against policies that trample upon the rights of political minorities.

On the surface it may appear that because of the value placed upon freedom and democracy by Americans, judicial dictatorship poses the gravest risk to the American governing system. The risk of majority tyranny is tempered by the fact that political minorities have the opportunity to lobby legislatures, to vote in elections, to run for office, and to cultivate the understanding of elected officials. Even if they cannot always achieve their goals, they can protect themselves by participating in democratic processes and publicizing instances in which individuals' rights are infringed by undesirable governmental policies. By contrast, there are no apparent checks upon federal judges who wish to pursue their own interests in shaping public policy. The judges are in office for life and the public cannot replace them for improperly influencing public policy. The perception that judicial dictatorship poses a grave threat to democracy is deceptive, however, because it ignores the many limitations upon judicial action that stem from the courts' connections to the political system. If judges were truly independent, unrestrained actors who could exercise their power as they wished, there would indeed be serious risks that judicial policy-making would disrupt the American democracy. But judges do not enjoy such unfettered power. The judicial system is a component of the larger political system. The political nature of courts imposes constraints upon judges. Therefore, judicially influenced public policy is not imposed upon American government and society but is instead a product of and continually shaped and limited by the political processes of the American governing system.

Judicial Selection and the Composition of the Judiciary

The process of selecting judges serves to provide voters and elected officials with the opportunity to constrain judicial policy-making by controlling the composition of the judiciary. In the federal court system, judges are appointed by the president and confirmed by the Senate. The president seeks to appoint judges whose views about judicial policy-making comport with those of the president's administration and political party. For example, President Reagan and his supporters were unhappy with the judicial policy-making undertaken by appointees of previous presidents. The Reagan administration curbed this trend by consciously screening candidates according to their support for specific public policies and their opposition to previously established judicial policies. If the judiciary begins to move too fast or too far in its decision making, the president can pull judicial decisions back toward the political center through the gradual process of appointing new kinds of judges when the incumbents die, retire, or resign. Because the president is selected through nationwide elections, the process of selecting judges gradually tracks, in a very rough fashion, the general policy preferences expressed by the electorate. When the voters change directions and select a new president from a different political party, judicial appointments will gradually reflect those different values as well. The federal judiciary may be tied to an earlier era and outdated policy preferences when the country undergoes a dramatic political shift,[10] as when Franklin Roosevelt's liberal New Deal coalition gained power in the 1930s and the holdover justices on the Supreme Court systematically invalidated Roosevelt's economic regulation and social welfare legislation. The infusion of new appointees will, however, eventually lead the courts to move in the direction of evolving societal changes as demonstrated by the switch in Supreme Court decisions as Roosevelt began appointing new justices in 1937. Thus, the judicial selection process helps to keep the judiciary's composition and judges' decisions from deviating too far from the general preferences expressed by voters in periodic elections.

Judicial selection methods and the composition of courts also limit the risks of excessive judicial influence over public policy in state judicial systems. Many states select their judges through partisan or nonpartisan elections.[11] In states with electoral systems, the voters have the opportunity to replace judicial officers whose decisions are regarded as too extreme or as exerting inappropriate influence over public policy. Other states employ appointment processes in which governors or legislators select judges, usually from a list of nominees presented by judicial nominating commissions.[12] Governors, legislatures, and selection committees will seek to appoint new judges who possess an appropriately restrained conception of judicial power, especially if they believe that previous appointees have pushed the limits of judicial authority beyond proper boundaries.

Judicial appointees in both the federal and state systems are drawn from the mainstream of American society and have succeeded in mainstream party politics. Normally, lawyers cannot become judges through either appointment or election unless they have been active in politics and cultivated relationships with important leaders in one of the major political parties. Because they are products of the mainstream political system, judges are unlikely to bring policy preferences to the bench that are wholly different from those possessed by large segments of the American public. Very few judges are likely to be radical reformers who pursue an extremist policy agenda. Judges are generally affluent political elites whose values and interests favor the maintenance of the general policy preferences of their historical era. Thus, the policy outcomes produced by judicial decisions are likely to be quite similar to the policy initiatives advocated by other political actors. Although judicial policy decisions may be controversial and generate opposition, the underlying controversies do not generally reflect unique or idiosyncratic policy preferences possessed by judges. Instead, the controversies and attendant condemnations of judicial policy-making reflect deep divisions within American society when there is no public consensus about which policy to pursue. During the 1970s and 1980s, courts were harshly criticized for their decisions affecting such issues as abortion, affirmative action, and school desegregation. In each instance, although substantial segments of the public opposed these judicial decisions, other large segments of society supported the policy preferences advanced by the judiciary.

Judges' Role Conceptions and Self-Restraint

Judges do not merely follow their personal policy preferences in deciding cases. Policy preferences are an important factor underlying judicial decisions,[13] but judges also constrain their personal values when they believe that the expression of such preferences is inappropriate within judicial decision-making. Research on decision making by appellate judges indicates that judges' conceptions of the proper judicial role can limit the breadth of their decisions. If judges view themselves as "Interpreters" or "Realists" instead of "Innovators," they will weigh very carefully the propriety and anticipated consequences of any policy-influencing decision.[14] Although a judge may believe that a particular policy would be "best for society," he or she may decline to advance that policy through a judicial decision because of a belief that policy-making concerning the issue in question is appropriately reserved for the legislative and executive branches of government.

Judges' theories of constitutional and statutory interpretation may be components of this self-restraint based upon a conception of the judiciary's proper role. For example, proponents of constitutional interpretation according to the original intent of the framers argue that their method of interpretation consciously attempts to limit opportunities for judges to influence public policy through the application of personal values.[15] Theoretically, by following the framers' intentions, judges will all follow the same consistent principles. Although interpretation by original intent is fraught with difficulties,[16] abandoned by proponents in selected cases,[17] and still can result in judicial influence over public policy, the application of this and other legal theories illustrates that the means employed by judges to shape their decisions can limit the range of possible decisions. Judges can restrain their policy preferences in deference to a particular theory of judicial interpretation.

The self-restraint exercised by judicial officers may reflect not only their sense of the proper exercise of authority under the constitutional system but also their concern about the judiciary's image in the eyes of the public. The power of the judicial branch is regarded as flowing from its reputation as a "legal" rather than a "political" institution. Judicial officers who are concerned about the judiciary's image may restrain their own decision making in order to preserve the courts' legitimacy. The preservation of judicial legitimacy is premised on the practical expectation that people will be less likely to obey legal decisions voluntarily if they do not regard judges' opinions as proper, legitimate pronouncements based upon law rather than upon politics. Justice Felix Frankfurter articulated the most well-known warning to the judiciary regarding the maintenance of its image:

> The Court's authority—possessed neither of purse nor sword—ultimately rests on sustained public confidence in its moral sanction. Such feeling must be nourished by the Court's complete detachment, in fact and in appearance, from political entanglements and by abstention from injecting itself into the class of political forces in political settlements.[18]

Although Justice Frankfurter's restraintist sentiments are from an earlier era, self-restraint continues to affect decisions in contemporary courts. The Reagan administration made a concerted effort to appoint as new federal judges only those Republicans who expressed support for the administration's views on the necessity of judicial self-restraint.[19] Although the Reagan appointees have, at times, pursued their own policy preferences,[20] their expressed views on restraint may limit the range of their decision-making options.

The notion that many judges constrain their own decisions affecting public policy does not provide much reassurance that the judiciary will not engage in dictatorial behavior. Self-restraint is, however, merely one of several elements that serve to place boundaries around the expression of policy preferences by judges.

The Structure of Courts

The potential for dictatorial judicial decisions is lessened by the hierarchical structure of the state and federal court systems. If lower court judges' decisions go beyond certain boundaries, those decisions will be overruled on appeal by appellate courts. One of the functions of the appeals process is to create uniformity in judicial decisions within an appellate jurisdiction and thereby to prevent excessive creativity or unwarranted assertions of judicial power by individual judges.

In addition, the U.S. Supreme Court, state supreme courts, and other appellate courts are constrained by their structures as collegial judicial bodies containing several judges. No single judge can determine outcomes in appellate cases. The judges must compromise, persuade, and otherwise interact with their colleagues in order to develop a stable majority coalition for each decision. The process of interacting with and pleasing other judges inevitably limits the scope of potential decisions because extreme viewpoints must be moderated and compromised in order to attract the support of other judges. The likelihood that any particular decision will go "too far" is lessened by the fact that all decisions must satisfy the role orientations and sense of propriety of a majority of judges within the appellate court. The U.S. Supreme Court's nine-member size insures that the ultimate review and decision in legal cases involves the agreement of at least five justices. Because very few presidents will enjoy the opportunity to appoint five justices, judicial decisions in the Supreme Court frequently must please justices who were appointed by different presidents and whose views were shaped by different historical eras in order to garner majority support. President Franklin Roosevelt was the last president to have five of his appointees serve simultaneously on the Supreme Court. Because subsequent presidents have been limited to two terms in office by the Twenty-Second Amendment, it is less likely that many presidents will gain the opportunity to load the Court with appointees who represent a single set of policy preferences. In addition, because justices' decisions frequently deviate from the expectations of the president who appoint them, a president who attempts to foster a precise judicial policy agenda is likely to be disappointed with at least some Supreme Court decisions.

External Constraints

Because the judicial branch is a component of the political system rather than a separate entity, judicial policy-making is affected by interactions with other branches of government. When courts issue decisions, other political actors react, especially if judicial decisions conflict with the policy goals of outside political institutions. The judges are cognizant of the power of other governmental and political actors and thus judicial decisions may be limited by judges' anticipation of reactions from external political forces.

Legislatures can take several steps to react against judicial decisions. When judges interpret statutes in a manner with which legislators disagree, the legislators can directly modify the judicial decision by enacting new legislation that clarifies the meaning of the statute in question. In 1988, for example, Congress passed the Civil Rights Restoration Act to reverse a Supreme Court decision that had limited the coverage of a gender discrimination statute aimed at colleges and universities.[21] As with other disputes between Congress and the Supreme Court, legislators will continue to initiate new laws as long as they are unhappy with statutory interpretations produced by the judiciary.

Congress also initiates constitutional amendments when it is unhappy with judicial decisions. In the aftermath of judicial decisions on abortion, school prayer, school desegregation, and other controversial matters, members of Congress have proposed constitutional amendments that would alter the judicial interpretations of the Constitution. Although recent efforts to amend the Constitution have not succeeded, there have been several occasions in history when the amendment process has successfully nullified Supreme Court decisions.[22] The Sixteenth Amendment, which approved federal income taxation in 1913, overruled a Supreme Court decision which struck down Congressional efforts to implement an income tax by statute.[23] The ratification of the Twenty-Sixth Amendment, which lowered the voting age to eighteen, also followed a Supreme Court decision that prevented a statutory implementation of the new policy.[24]

Congress also has attempted to enact legislation to limit the judiciary's jurisdiction over issues in which legislators disagree with court decisions. Although there was one notable example after the Civil War when the Supreme Court acquiesced to a Congressional withdrawal of appellate jurisdiction,[25] this method of constraining judicial policy-making has not directly affected the judiciary. Members of Congress are reluctant to tamper with courts' jurisdiction and there are lingering questions about the constitutional propriety of complete withdrawals of jurisdiction over issues—questions that judges themselves will examine and decide if such statutes are ever passed. The threat of altered jurisdictions, although not frequently exercised, may deter judges from forthrightly advancing policy preferences that clash with legislative preferences. During the 1950s, for example, the Supreme Court issued a controversial decision that limited Congressional authority to conduct hearings to investigate American communists[26] as well as other decisions affecting the issue of internal security.

Two years later, the Court appeared to modify its position in order to grant Congress greater power in such investigations.[27] Many commentators have attributed the change in the Supreme Court's decisions to the threat of jurisdiction-curbing legislation initiated in Congress during the intervening period:

> Bills were introduced aimed at the Court's rulings on internal security matters such as legislative investigations, the executive's loyalty-security programs, state control of teachers and admission of lawyers to the practice of law, and federal preemption of state internal subversion legislation. None of the bills passed, although the Senate vote was very close (a one-vote margin) and the Court appeared to retreat in the face of the attack.[28]

The president may pressure the judiciary by advocating or proposing legislation and constitutional amendments designed to limit judicial policy-making. In the most famous presidential threat to the Supreme Court, Franklin Roosevelt, who was unhappy with the Court's obstruction of his legislative programs, proposed that the Supreme Court be structured to permit the president to appoint an additional justice whenever a serving justice reached the age of seventy. The immediate effect of the proposal would have been to permit Roosevelt to make six new appointments and instantly change the balance of power on a Supreme Court that would grow to fifteen members under the plan. Although Roosevelt's plan encountered significant political opposition, the political confrontation was defused when Justice Owen Roberts changed his position on economic regulation issues, the so-called "switch in time that saved nine," and thereby placed the Court in line with the nation's legislative policy developments. Soon thereafter, justices began to retire from the Court and Roosevelt replaced them with his own political supporters.[29] The political threat facing the institution of the Supreme Court may very well have led Justice Roberts and perhaps other justices to reconsider their opposition to the policy preferences advanced by the elected branches of government.

Concerns About Compliance

Because judges have limited ability to implement and enforce their decisions, judicial policy-making is constrained by judges' anticipation of adverse public reactions. During the Supreme Court's deliberations in *Brown v. Board of Education*, for example, the justices' policy preferences for dismantling racial segregation were constrained by their twin desires to maximize the legitimacy of their pronouncement through a unanimous decision and to implement the decision gradually to avoid excessive social upheaval.[30] As a result, the initial *Brown* decision in 1954 was a general policy declaration with great symbolic effect but few immediate practical consequences.[31] The second *Brown* decision in 1955 concerning implementation required only that schools be desegregated with "all deliberate speed" rather than with dramatic, immediate reforms.[32] The justices' concerns about adverse public reactions limited both the formulation and impact of their policy decision.

Judges must also produce judicial decisions that executive branch officials will be willing to obey and enforce. For example, after early Supreme Court decisions favoring the protection of the Cherokee Nation's rights and property against encroachment by whites in Georgia, President Andrew Jackson refused to enforce the decisions. As a result, the Native Americans were forcibly marched to Oklahoma, with hundreds dying along the way, despite the fact that they had prevailed in court.[33] Jackson is reported to have said "Well, [Chief Justice] John Marshall has made his decision, now let him enforce it."[34] Jackson's statement and actions provide an extreme example of the practical concerns about enforcement that may limit judges' policy-making decisions. If there is noncompliance with court decisions, judges can issue additional judicial orders but they must rely on governors and presidents to supply law enforcement personnel to ensure that judicial orders are implemented. The implementation decision in the second *Brown v. Board of Education* decision may have been guided by the justices' concern for the existence and degree of presidential support that would underlie enforcement of the controversial judicial decision. The *amicus* brief submitted by the Solicitor General on behalf of the Eisenhower administration contained the phrase "all deliberate speed" and the justices, in adopting the phrase, may have viewed the brief as containing a signal that President Eisenhower would be willing to enforce the decision but perhaps not on an immediate, massive scale.[35] Indeed, despite his general lack of concern about racial equality,[36] Eisenhower eventually deployed military forces in order to ensure that nine African-American students would be allowed to attend Central High School in Little Rock, Arkansas in the face of violent white opposition.

Conclusion: The Legitimacy of Judicial Policy-Making

There is no escape from the troubling questions raised by the continuing involvement of courts in shaping public policy. Because the limits of judicial authority are not precisely defined in the Constitution and because there is disagreement within society about the proper role of courts, policy-shaping actions by judges will continue to generate controversy. There is no easy way to evaluate the legitimacy of judicial policy-making. Assessments about the legitimacy of judicial policy-making and the proper limitations upon judges' decisions involve evaluative judgments about the nature of the Constitution and the risks posed by judicial policy-making. Simplistic denunciations of judicial policy-making as always illegitimate or entirely dictatorial tend to ignore the constitutional bases for such decisions in the judicial responsibility for interpreting and enforcing the Bill of Rights. Blanket denunciations also usually ignore the court system's political characteristics which elicit, affect, and limit judges' decisions. Broad condemnations of judicial policy-making may emanate from critics who disagree with the specific policy preferences advanced by judicial decisions. Similarly, reactive defenders of judicial policy-making may focus upon the policy results that they favor rather than the underlying constitutional issues. The legitimacy of judicial policy-making cannot be judged by merely assessing the policy outcomes produced by the courts. For example, in the early twentieth century, Supreme Court justices actively shaped conservative policies by preventing legislatures from regulating the economy and initiating social welfare programs. In the mid-twentieth century, a new generation of justices shaped liberal policies aimed at various social problems. An endorsement of judicial policy-making based upon the outcomes in one era may lead to grave discomfort when judges in a later era utilize their policy-making "license" to drive society in a contrary direction.

As demonstrated by the continuing debates about the legitimacy of judicial policy-making, there is plenty of room for disagreement about how extensive judges' power over public policy should be. Fundamentally, however, there can be no question that *some* influence over public policy by courts is both proper and inevitable. In a constitutional system that authorizes independent judges to make law through their power to interpret constitutions, statutes, and prior cases, political interests will inevitably utilize courts as forums to pursue policy objectives. Moreover, because the American system places the selection of judges under the control of partisan political actors (i.e., elected officials and political parties), political interests will inevitably seek to advance their policy preferences by striving to place like-minded partisans into judgeships. These connections between courts and politics may dismay those who fear improper or dictatorial policy-making actions by judges, but it is these very connections themselves that insure that judges remain connected to mainstream society and that judicial decisions remain within the evolving boundaries established by the interactions between courts and other political institutions. Although debates will continue concerning the propriety of specific decisions by individual judges that may indeed go "too far" in the eyes of many observers, it is reasonable to conclude as a general matter that judicial policy-making is both legitimate and constrained as an inevitable product of the American constitutional governing system.

CHAPTER 3
THE CAPACITY OF COURTS AS POLICY-MAKING FORUMS

IN ANY GIVEN CASE, QUESTIONS may be raised about whether it is proper under the American system of government for courts to influence the development of public policy. This issue about the legitimacy of judicial policy-making is not, however, the only fundamental controversy underlying the role of courts in policy formulation and implementation. There is also a continuing debate regarding courts' capabilities for producing public policy. Even if it is legitimate for courts to affect public policy, do they have the necessary resources and characteristics to formulate and implement policy? In essence, are courts structured to be capable forums for good policy decisions? As noted by Donald Horowitz, the issues of courts' legitimacy and capacity for policy-making are related:

> [The issue is not] whether the courts *should* perform certain tasks but . . . whether they *can* perform [those tasks] competently.
> Of course, legitimacy and capacity are related. A court wholly without capacity may forfeit its claim to legitimacy. A court wholly without legitimacy will soon suffer from diminished capacity.[1]

Questions about courts' legitimacy and capacity can be examined separately, but both elements need to exist for effective judicial policy-making.

Social science research on judicial decision making has shown that judicial decisions are shaped by the same kinds of personal and political influences that affect decisions in other branches of government. Judges' decisions are not dictated by "law." Judges use legal precedents and theories in their written opinions to justify the decisions that they make, but their attitudes, values, political ideologies, and policy preferences exert significant influence over their decisions. For example, scholars who study the Supreme Court have concluded that justices' "policy preferences serve as a powerful force shaping how they view cases and choose among alternative policies."[2] Studies of other courts demonstrate a strong correlation between judges' political party affiliations and the decisions that they make on civil rights and other cases.[3] Republican and Democratic judges tend to decide cases differently because they possess differing attitudes, values, and policy preferences. Although these political influences that shape judicial decision making are similar to the underlying influences that affect legislators and executive branch officials, decision-making processes within the judicial branch are structured differently than parallel processes in other governmental institutions. The judicial process involves different actors and different kinds of information. Decision makers in the judiciary possess role conceptions and authority that differ from those of elected officials. The 1950s, 1960s, and 1970s were decades of swiftly accelerating policy-making activities by judges. In the aftermath of those decades, some commentators believe that courts did not go far enough, but others believe, in the words of one critic, "the dream of the 1960s and 70s that activist courts can be the agents of social progress has worn very thin."[4] The contradictory assessments of the consequences of judicial policy-making frequently stem from divergent analyses of the capacity of the judiciary to develop and implement beneficial public policies.

Arguments Endorsing Courts as Good Policy-Making Forums

In a well-known article in the *Harvard Law Review*, Abram Chayes presented several arguments advancing the idea that the judiciary may have some important institutional advantages for policy-making tasks.[5] Although Chayes was not alone in raising the idea that courts may be well-suited to the task of policy-making, his arguments provide a good illustration of the justifications presented on behalf of courts' policy-making capacity.

Courts are arguably good forums for policy-making because judges are, relative to other governmental officials, insulated from interest groups, political parties, and other direct partisan political influences. In the federal courts in particular, judges do not need to worry about reelection. Unlike other actors within the governing system, federal judges are structurally positioned to undertake the course of action that they see as most beneficial to society without any significant personal risk from political backlash. Moreover, judges have a traditional role of striving to be as neutral as possible when considering competing arguments. Although systematic examination of judicial decisions by social scientists can provide evidence that judges' attitudes, values, and policy preferences influence outcomes, judges consciously try to be as fair as they can be when making decisions. Judicial officers' heightened consciousness about striving for fairness contrasts sharply with the motivations of legislators and executive branch officials who openly curry favor with interest groups, voters, and other political constituencies that can help elected officials to gain and maintain power within government.

Judges can develop *ad hoc* policies that are tailored to remedy particular problematic situations. Legislatures' policy decisions tend to sweep with a broad stroke across all relevant situations without regard for the subtle but potentially important differences between specific circumstances. By contrast, judges can take particular situational needs and constraints into consideration in carefully designing remedial policies that address specific problems.

The judicial process permits a relatively high degree of participation from interested parties. Unlike the legislative process in which poor and unorganized interests are not represented at all by lobbyists, both sides in a court case are generally represented by professional legal counsel. Additional arguments and evidence may be presented through *amicus* briefs and expert witnesses so that the judge will have access to viewpoints and evidence from all relevant perspectives.

The adversarial structure of the judicial process creates incentives for both sides to bring forward as much favorable information as possible. In the legislative context, sometimes only specific interest groups have the resources and opportunity to testify at legislative hearings in order to make their views heard by legislators. Similarly, administrative agencies within the executive branch are noted for responding to organized political interest groups but not to individual citizens. By contrast, both parties in a court case will bring forward all available favorable information so that the judge can sift through complete presentations of the competing arguments and evidence before rendering a decision. Because attorneys for both parties have ethical and personal incentives to represent their clients zealously in order to win the case, they will leave no stone unturned in bringing relevant information to the court's attention.

Unlike legislative and administrative governmental forums, courts must respond to the issues brought before them. The policy agendas of judges are determined by the cases initiated in court and judges do not have the same ability as other governmental officials to avoid certain difficult questions while consciously pursuing favored policy issues. Legislators ignore intractable problems and address issues of interest that will generate political benefits for them among the electorate. Judges tackle intractable policy problems because parties bring such issues to court and ask the judiciary to develop solutions. In addition, the judges who hear the complete arguments and evidence are the decision makers in court. Unlike the processes in the legislative and executive branches in which arguments, evidence, and decisions are filtered through layers of different offices and staff personnel, the judicial process provides a relatively non-bureaucratic setting for policy-making decisions.

Arguments Opposing Courts as Effective Policy-Making Forums

Donald Horowitz presented the best known critique of courts' capacity for effective policy-making in his book, *The Courts and Social Policy*.[6] Horowitz examined judicial interventions into state and local governmental institutions to highlight the drawbacks affecting judges' effectiveness as policymakers.

Judges cannot select their areas of policy emphasis and, because of the constant flow of their other judicial responsibilities, they cannot give sustained attention to specific issues. Although legislative committees and executive agencies contain experts on various policy issues, judges are not likely to be experts on any public policy issues. Judges are generalists trained in law who gained authority over public policy issues by virtue of becoming judicial officers. Judges are also insulated from the environment affected by their policy decisions because judicial ethics require that judges withdraw from participation in most social and political organizations. Legislators meet regularly with constituents to keep in touch with public opinion and social concerns. Judges keep to themselves within the protective confines of the courthouse. Because they lack expertise and close contacts with affected communities, judges are less able to anticipate the broader consequences of their decisions. Moreover, the *ad hoc* nature of judicial decisions creates policies that lack the comprehensive, coherent perspective that may be developed in legislative and executive settings through the utilization of policy studies, experts, and long-term planning.

Judges' policy decisions are based upon a skewed sample of problems. Judges address the particular case that happens to arrive before them. The case may be highly unrepresentative of the larger problems affecting that policy issue, yet the specific circumstances underlying the case in question may become the basis for policy decisions that produce detrimental effects upon a variety of other cases. In addition, the issue addressed by the judge is framed by litigants in accordance with their particularistic interests. Therefore the judge has little ability to take a comprehensive view of the policy problem, even if he or she desires to do so. In the adversarial process, the parties have an incentive to hide unfavorable information and the judge does not have a large enough staff to ferret out complete information. Thus, the judge's decision relies upon the potentially biased and incomplete information submitted by the competing parties. Moreover, even if comprehensive information is obtained, the judge may not be able to utilize relevant information because of constraints imposed by decisions of higher appellate courts that have limited the range of judicial policy choices in a specific issue area.[7]

The process of litigation itself may be an undesirable means to formulate and adjust public policy. Litigation leads to definitive decisions in favor of one party or the other. Such "win or lose" decisions may be an undesirable means of addressing many policy issues. Policy outcomes derived from negotiation and compromise may provide more satisfactory and socially beneficial solutions for society's problems. Thus legislative bodies containing representatives from various segments of society are better suited to develop compromise policies that will gain broad acceptance.

Assessing Courts' Capacity as Policy-Making Forums

The foregoing summaries are cast as competing sets of arguments about courts' capacity (or lack thereof) for producing good public policy outcomes. In fact, most authors, including Chayes and Horowitz, discuss the complexity of the capacity issue in greater detail. Yet, these simplified arguments represent the underlying basis for raging disagreements about the effectiveness of judicial policy-making. Which set of arguments concerning judges' capacity for effective policy-making is closest to the mark? Both viewpoints contain accurate elements, but neither fully captures the actual complex interactions that underlie judicial policy making.

Characterization of Issues

One characteristic of judicial policy-making is that issues must undergo a "legalization" process in the hands of lawyers before they can be presented in court. Legal procedures are structured to address issues that fit within the confines of specific dispute categories. Because disputes that do not fit within a recognized basis for legal action cannot be heard by courts, people must transform their claims into legal forms that courts are willing to consider. As Horowitz observes, "[t]he framing of the issue is geared to the litigant and his complaint," which may represent an atypical case, rather than to the broad policy issue that may be affected by a judicial decision.[8] It is necessary to create a narrow focus in litigation for the presentation of evidence and the analysis of issues, and this narrowing process of transforming claims into legal actions may limit the ability of judges to give broad consideration to a policy question. When a homosexual man challenged on privacy grounds the constitutionality of Georgia's law that provides for sentences of up to twenty years in prison for sodomy, even if between consenting adults or married couples within the privacy of their own bedrooms, the majority of justices on the Supreme Court characterized the issue very narrowly: "Does a homosexual have a constitutional right to commit sodomy?"[9] Because of the way the issue was framed, the Court did not consider broadly whether or not such a law represents a good policy. Indeed, after deciding against the claimant, one justice's opinion implicitly informed the claimant that if he had challenged the law as having an excessively severe punishment, the justice might have decided the case differently.[10] Obviously, the justices assessed the policy in accordance with a very narrow characterization of the legal issue (i.e., privacy rights of homosexuals) rather than from a broad perspective that considered the law's impact on heterosexuals and the potentially "cruel and unusual" nature of the punishment. Ideally, policymakers should examine an issue comprehensively and not analyze it from one limited, selected angle.

The legalization process also casts policy debates into a framework of individual constitutional "rights." By examining policy decisions as if they are absolute entitlements for individuals, the courts may lack the capacity for flexible development of policy outcomes that maximize the interests of competing actors or that benefit society as a whole.[11] In addition, a "rights" orientation may permit interest groups to capture a public policy issue and thereby control executive branch agencies' ability to administer governmental programs in the interest of society. According to Jeremy Rabkin:

When different constituencies can challenge so many different aspects of agency operations, private rights or "legally protected interests" no longer seem to be an exception from the general flow of public policy, but rather the essential elements of public policy themselves. In other words, public policy seems to reduce to the legally protected claims of contending groups.[12]

Although this observation raises a serious concern about courts' capacity for comprehensive policy-making, it must be considered in light of the capabilities of other governmental branches. Legislative and executive branch actions are not focused upon individuals' "rights," but they are equally susceptible to capture by narrow interest groups. In theory, the accountability of elected officials to the voters will undercut the power of political action committees, interest group lobbying, and close relationships between organized interests and executive branch agencies. In practice, however, many policies produced by legislative and executive decisions are narrowly tailored for specific interests. Thus the risks of narrow policy-making by courts are less compelling as evidence of judicial incapacity. Moreover, as discussed in chapter 2, the political system provides constraints upon courts that limit the extent to which judicial policy-making may remain uniquely captured by any particular interest.

The legalization process creates opportunities for judges to avoid cases that are initiated in court. Although judges have tackled many difficult issues, they are able to utilize jurisdictional concepts such as "standing," "mootness," and "political question doctrine" to avoid issues that might generate excessive political controversy. When judges focus upon a litigant's "standing," they question whether this is the proper party to initiate a case and they challenge the litigant's assertion that there was a sufficient injury to meet legal standards for litigation. When he was a circuit court of appeals judge, current Supreme Court Justice Antonin Scalia avoided making decisions on civil rights issues by questioning whether claimants had the proper legal basis for initiating a lawsuit.[13] The issue of "mootness" arises if the case's underlying conflict has ended before the courts have fully considered the case. When the first affirmative action case arrived at the Supreme Court in *DeFunis v. Odegaard*,[14] the justices avoided the issue by declaring it moot because the plaintiff had subsequently been accepted into the law school that he was suing for "reverse discrimination." Although affirmative action was a divisive issue, the Supreme Court managed to delay its contact with the controversial issue. The "political question" doctrine has served as a basis of judicial avoidance of many matters, particularly in the area of foreign policy, when the courts declare that the issue should properly be addressed by the legislative and executive branches of government.

How does the legalization process for policy issues affect courts' capacity for policy-making? By examining narrow issues there are risks that judges' will not analyze issues comprehensively and that the resulting judicial decisions will affect public policy in undesirable or unintended ways. At the same time, however, the legalization process creates opportunities for courts to avoid undertaking policy decisions or to limit the scope of decisions and thereby defer primary decision-making responsibility to the other branches of government.

Access to Information

The adversary system of courtroom combat between competing attorneys has been criticized for the risk it creates that relevant information will not be presented to judges. Although both competing parties are represented by attorneys, the attorneys control the information that is presented to the court. The two parties in the case present all relevant information that is favorable to their cause. They hope that the other side will fail to discover and present information that might to detrimental to their arguments. Thus, the judges may not have access to complete information. As described by Marvin Frankel:

> While the administration of justice is designated as the public's business and the decisionmakers are public people (whether full-time judges or lay judges who sit in jury boxes), the process is initiated, shaped, and managed by the private contestants in civil matters. . . . The deciders, though commissioned to discover the truth, are passive recipients, not active explorers. They take what they are given. They consider the questions raised by counsel, rarely any others.[15]

By contrast, the German legal system empowers judges to perform as the primary investigators who question witnesses, seek additional evidence, and otherwise actively pursue complete information.[16]

In addition, judges are not experts on the public policy issues that they shape with their decisions. There are inevitably questions about whether "generalist" judges have the capacity to make good decisions on complex policy issues. Moreover, because judges frequently rely upon "theoretical knowledge" from social scientists' studies, they cannot accurately predict the consequences of their policy decisions.[17] Although these are important criticisms to direct at judicial policy-making, do they indicate that courts are incapable of making good policy decisions? Might these same criticisms be directed at other governmental institutions that shape public policy?

Legislatures presumably have access to broader information than courts because issues are not characterized to fit the contours of law and the interests of two specific litigants. In addition, legislatures benefit from the assistance of committee staff members who possess expertise on various policy issues. Legislatures can also hear testimony and receive reports from a wide range of experts without regard for narrow rules of evidence that limit the kinds of information regarded as admissible in court. Although these attributes appear to grant significant advantages to legislatures as policy-making forums, in fact, courts share many of these attributes.

As Stephen Wasby points out, legislatures frequently examine policy issues on a case-by-case basis when a particular problem rises to the top of the legislative policy agenda because of a specific event or circumstance that captures public attention.[18] Thus legislatures do not undertake public policy decisions from a comprehensive perspective either. John Kingdon's research on the policy process in the legislative and executive branches indicates that:

> Problems are often not self-evident by the indicators. They need a little push to get the attention of people in and around government. That push is often provided by a focusing event like a crisis or disaster that comes along to call attention to the problem, a powerful symbol that catches on, or the personal experience of a policy maker.[19]

Judicial policy-making arises from authoritative attention to a specific dispute between two or more contending parties, but legislative policy-making may be initiated and shaped by similar circumstances.

In the legislative context, legislators are "generalists" who make decisions with the advice of experts. Similarly, judges utilize the advice of experts to make decisions. The contending parties bring expert witnesses to court, but the judge may also listen to separate experts or appoint "special masters," frequently college professors or attorneys with specific expertise, to provide advice or oversight for difficult policy disputes.[20] Thus judges have the authority to seek additional information in order to examine issues more comprehensively. Whether or not they actually examine policy disputes from a broad perspective is determined by the actions of the judges and litigants in specific cases. The same is true, however, of legislative decisions because legislators often listen only to representatives and experts from selected interest groups before enacting legislation with wide impact.

Although judges are criticized for failing to predict accurately the consequences of their policy decisions, other policy-making institutions are similarly flawed in their capacity to predict effectively the long-term results of particular public policy initiatives.[21] Legislatures and executive branch agencies also rely upon "theoretical knowledge" from social scientists' studies and therefore, like courts, must wait to see the practical effects of public policy decisions.

It is easy to criticize courts for ineffective policy-making by examining persistent policy problems that have received judicial attention. An accurate assessment of courts' capacity for policy-making can only be gained, however, by examining additional criteria that critics of the courts often fail to evaluate. According to Wasby, analysis of judicial capacity requires attention to both the *comparative capacity* of courts and other policy-making institutions and the *will to proceed* that is characteristic of a particular policy-shaping actor.[22] From a comparative perspective, courts share many of the capacity-reducing disabilities that are characteristic in alternative policy-making forums. In addition, because of their independence from direct control by voters, federal judges, in particular, may have a greater capacity for tackling rather than avoiding difficult controversies.

The Policy-Shaping Process

Critics of judicial capacity assert that judicial policy-making is undesirable because court decisions favor one party or the other for policy issues in which negotiation and compromise may be most desirable. This image of the formal judicial process does not, however, accurately reflect the processes of judicial policy-making for most cases. The adversarial litigants do not conduct their case preparations in isolation and then meet in a "clash of gladiators" in the courtroom. The actual process of civil litigation is more accurately characterized as "bargaining in the shadow of the law."[23] Lawyers for the contending parties meet continuously throughout the months of preparation for trial in order to obtain information from each other in the pretrial process known as "discovery." Judges encourage and even force the parties to negotiate with each other in an effort to reach a settlement without a judicial decision. The parties "bargain in the shadow of the law" because the threat of a zero-sum decision looms over their heads as the scheduled trial date approaches. Thus most civil cases are processed through negotiated settlements and relatively few cases actually receive judicial decisions after a trial.

47

Because of the importance of behind-the-scenes negotiation in the civil litigation process, judges are not merely potential policymakers through their authority to issue judicial decisions, they are also policy shapers through their ability to encourage negotiation between the parties. One well-known article about the role of judges in reforming governmental institutions characterized judges as "power-brokers" who make choices about how to guide the judicial processing of policy disputes.[24] Observers have noted judges' increasing emphasis upon negotiation rather than litigation as the means for processing disputes. Indeed, contemporary judicial officers have been labeled as "managerial judges" because they "are meeting with parties in chambers to encourage settlement of disputes and to supervise case preparation. Both before and after trial, judges are playing a critical role in shaping litigation and influencing results."[25]

The negotiation process that underlies judicial policy-making creates opportunities for participation by contending parties in the development of compromise policy outcomes that avoid the necessity of a single judge making a choice about the most desirable public policy. A negotiation process may have advantages over other kinds of policy-shaping processes by encouraging presentation of complete information and by inducing opposing interests to work together in formulating results that will receive broad support. Studies of judicial policy-making have found that judges utilize negotiation to shape and refine policy outcomes. For example, in Alabama, a federal judge took control of the state's correctional institutions because, among other things, public health inspectors found the prisons to be unfit for human habitation.[26] A study of prison litigation in Alabama found that the state government and the prisoners' advocates engaged in continuing negotiations during the development and implementation of remedies.[27] In studies of judicial policy-making concerning several issue areas (i.e., prisons, mental health institutions, housing, school desegregation), Phillip Cooper found that judges played complex roles, which combined negotiation and adjudication, but that judges did not fit any simplistic characterization as judicial policymakers who simply issue decisions after an adversarial trial:

> [J]udges play different roles at different stages of a case. The judge plays a facilitator role in the first part of the remedy crafting process and a ratifier/developer role in the second. In the plan development and negotiation stage, all the judges [in the study] encouraged settlement or, at a minimum, a narrowing of issues. In each case . . . the judges found points at which they declared limits. When those limits were reached, the process became more

formal and the judges became less a facilitator and more a validator or ratifying official who placed the court's imprimatur on specific plans submitted by the parties without regard to voluntary acceptance by the other parties.[28]

The Consequences of Judicial Decisions

There are studies indicating that judges frequently do not foresee the adverse consequences of their decisions. One study, for example, indicates that judicial intervention in prison administration may exacerbate prison violence by altering the established procedures and authority structure within institutions.[29] Commentators also note that judicial policy-making often fails to accomplish intended objectives. In urban school desegregation cases, for example, some commentators argue that judicial intervention contributes to deterioration in city school systems as middle-class families leave the city to avoid court-mandated busing programs.[30] Does the existence of adverse consequences from judicial policy-making indicate that judges lack the capacity to formulate and implement effective policies? Or, do the less-than-completely-successful attempts at judicial policy-making simply indicate that judges' effectiveness is limited by the same kinds of factors that diminish the success of policy initiatives produced by other governmental branches? In fact, court-mandated school desegregation has been successful in increasing educational opportunity and reducing polarization in many communities, especially in county-wide school systems and medium-sized cities which contain a broad mixture of racial and socioeconomic groups.[31] The highly-publicized failures of busing programs in the largest cities stem, at least in part, from the Supreme Court's 1974 decision to limit such programs to the confines of rigid and relatively arbitrary established school system boundaries within metropolitan areas.[32] The slim five-member Supreme Court majority that constrained the range of desegregation remedies available to district judges was apparently concerned about the massive political backlash that would be generated if affluent suburbanites were forced to participate in developing solutions for the problems affecting predominantly minority urban school systems.[33] There is nothing unique about judges' inability to implement effective remedies for many of the significant problems of urban education. The legislative and executive branches of government have never effectively dealt with these pressing problems either. Judges, however, often feel a greater responsibility to do *something* to enforce constitutional rights when there is evidence that individuals are being victimized by discriminatory government policies and programs.

Implementation of Judicial Decisions

As indicated by the foregoing discussion, courts' capacity for producing good public policy outcomes is flawed. However, the flaws that afflict the judicial branch are not unique. In many respects, elements of the judicial policy-making process are similar to the processes undertaken in other branches (e.g., negotiatlon, assertion of narrow interests, etc.). Because they share common attributes with the judicial branch, the other branches of government cannot claim that they possess unique or flawless policy-making characteristics. Common weaknesses also exist in the policy implementation process. Public policy decisions are not self-implementing, whether they come from the Supreme Court, Congress, or the president. The president obviously has the greatest ability to implement decisions through control of the executive branch agencies that are responsible for administering governmental programs. However, even the executive branch's desires are affected by the actions of other political actors. As illustrated by the previous sections of this chapter, the inability of the judicial branch to implement public policy outcomes quickly and effectively should be viewed as a flaw with detrimental impacts upon the courts' policy-shaping capacity. This is a flaw that also affects other branches in various ways.

Although courts possess authority and legitimacy, and judicial decisions are enforceable as "law," judicial decisions often do not affect people's lives in the manner intended by the judges who issued those decisions. In 1990, for example, the Supreme Court issued a decision declaring that the Social Security Administration had violated a Congressional statute for sixteen years by refusing to pay benefits to children with a variety of disabilities including Down's syndrome, muscular dystrophy, spina bifida, AIDS, cystic fibrosis, and other chronic illnesses and birth defects.[34] Nine months after the Court's decision, the Social Security Administration had still not acted to pay benefits to the excluded children. Although children in these categories of illnesses and disabilities had prevailed in their policy dispute with the federal government by winning their case in the Supreme Court, they had not gained any benefits from their victory.[35] In such a case, any knowledgeable observer might guess that the children's goals were thwarted by the nature of government bureaucracies, which tend to change and implement policies very slowly. Indeed, this Social Security example is affected by the organizational characteristics of a large government bureaucracy. The difficulties that hinder the implementation of judicial decisions are more complex and pervasive than the simple bureaucratic inertia that is apparent in this example. Judicial policy decisions that affect other issues and actors must undergo a complex implementation process.

Because judicial decisions are not self-implementing, they must pass through the hands of various influential actors in the implementation process before they affect people's lives as public policies. The involvement of actors with varying political attitudes, values, and partisan interests can lead to inconsistent and unpredictable outcomes that diminish judicial officers' ability to ensure that policy decisions accomplish judges' intended goals. In a useful model for illustrating the implementation and impact of judicial policies, Charles Johnson and Bradley Canon identified interpreters, implementers, and consumers who, along with external political actors, determine precisely if and how judges' decisions will affect society.[36]

Interpreters

After judges issue a decision, the judicial opinion and its implications must be communicated and explained to the people who will carry it out. Police officers, for example, cannot follow closely the developing case law affecting search and seizure, *Miranda* warnings, and the other aspects of their jobs that are shaped by judicial decisions. Police officers do not have easy access to judges' opinions on such issues and they do not have the time or training to study and interpret the judges' intended meanings. Thus, other actors assume the task of interpreting and explaining judicial decisions.

The most far-reaching policy pronouncements come from the Supreme Court and other appellate courts. Frequently, if a trial judge makes a decision affecting public policy, the policy is not implemented until the issue has been examined by higher courts on appeal. When appellate courts issue policy decisions, their decisions are often limited to broad announcements that describe the duties of governmental officials or provide directions to officials involved within a particular case. Thus there is uncertainty about how the appellate decision is to apply to other cases with factual circumstances that are similar but not necessarily identical to the case decided by the appellate court. The interpretation and explanation of the judicial policy is developed gradually by the trial judges who must apply the appellate decision to the individual circumstances within new cases that arise concerning that policy issue. In *Brown v. Board of Education*, the Supreme Court explicitly acknowledged this interpretation and implementation process by instructing the federal district courts to examine alleged racial segregation within school systems and to develop remedies on a case-by-case basis. In other issue areas, the interpreting role of trial judges is equally inevitable but based on less explicit instructions. When the Supreme Court declared that criminal suspects must be informed of their rights prior to questioning in the *Miranda* decision,[37] trial judges subsequently had to decide precisely when the warnings had to be given, whether the warnings had to be phrased in a precise fashion, whether any questions could be asked of suspects prior to the warnings, and other issues that were not specifically spelled out in *Miranda*. Some of these issues received clarification from the Supreme Court in subsequent appeals, but because not all defendants fully pursue the appeal process or initiate other actions to challenge their convictions, the trial judges' interpretations frequently determined the outcomes of cases.

Other officials may also serve as interpreters. City attorneys advise police departments and school systems about the meaning and implications of judicial policy decisions. State attorneys general interpret decisions and provide instructions to state and local officials about how they must follow judicial policy pronouncements. Interpretation of judicial decisions is not always done by lawyers. Because of their positions within government agencies, people who are not trained in law may have to interpret and explain judicial policies. For example, police chiefs may interpret and explain decisions to patrol officers. School superintendents and principals may explain policies to teachers.

What are the consequences of this interpretation process? The various interpreters may interpret and explain the judicial policies in different ways. Moreover, some interpreters may never even hear about specific judicial decisions, especially if they are in small towns and do not have immediate access to the latest appellate opinions. Thus the actual meaning and implementation of the judicial policy may vary from city to city. The varying interpretations of the judges' intentions may stem from ambiguity in the wording of the judicial decision, mistaken perceptions on the part of interpreters, or even willful efforts by interpreters to shape the meaning of the judicial decision to fit the interpreter's own policy preferences. If city officials object to a judicial decision, they may intentionally interpret it as applying only to a limited range of circumstances. This may force a citizen to go back through the lengthy litigation process again in order to force the officials to follow a precise directive from the courts. In the meantime, the city officials have succeeded in weakening and delaying implementation of a policy that they oppose.

Implementers

Even if judicial policies are explained, they do not affect society according to the judges' intentions unless the officials responsible for carrying out the policies implement the directives properly. The *Miranda* decision, for example, is primarily a symbolic declaration unless police officers follow through with their instructions to inform suspects about the right to counsel and the right against self-incrimination. The success or failure of judicial policies can depend upon whether implementers have heard about the policies, whether they understood the explanations concerning the meaning of policy, and whether they comply with policy directives.

A failure to comply with judicial policies may stem from a lack of understanding or from an intentional effort to subvert the judicial policy. When federal courts issued orders to desegregate public schools, many schools systems in the South initially refused to comply. They knew what they were supposed to do, but the judicial policy did not take effect because the implementers disagreed with the policy and intentionally failed to follow the judges' directives. This willful noncompliance was premised upon a hope that other political actors, such as Congress, would combat the courts' decisions and prevent desegregation through a constitutional amendment or other means. Eventually, it took additional judicial decisions to levy fines on school systems, legislative and executive actions to withhold funds, and even the actions of law enforcement officers or military forces to initiate compliance in several cities.

Failure to implement judicial policies can occur in more subtle ways as well. For example, an individual police officer who makes an arrest in an alley with no witnesses present may have the opportunity to treat, or rather mistreat, the suspect in violation of judicial policies governing police behavior. If the suspect asserts that the police officer never informed him of his rights and the police officer says the suspect is lying, the judge will simply decide which witness is more credible. Such decisions are likely to go against a criminal suspect whether or not the suspect is telling the truth.

Alternatively, an individual police officer's failure to follow judicial policies in areas such as search and seizure is likely to stem from a lack of knowledge about the most recent, technical court decisions explaining the nuances of appropriate police behavior. Police cannot be expected to read and understand the most recent judicial decisions, especially because certain areas of law are refined every year by new decisions. There are likely to be weaknesses in the processes for communicating the details of judges' decisions to implementers and these weaknesses will reduce the effectiveness of judicial policies.

Consumers

The people directly affected by court decisions can also influence their implementation. Consumers may hear about important judicial policy decisions that are reported by the news media, but frequently they have no ability to learn about the most recent court cases. Thus, if the implementers fail to respect the consumers' rights in accordance with judicial directives and the consumers do not realize that their rights have been violated, the judicial policy will not be effectuated because there is no one to complain about the lack of implementation. For example, if a public school teacher in a small town leads prayers in the classroom in violation of the Supreme Court's 1962 decision in *Engel v. Vitale*[38] but no students or parents realize that this is improper, no one will complain and seek enforcement of the judicial policy. In addition, if a consumer recognizes a rights violation but is frustrated by resistance from a school system or other government agency, or alternatively, cannot afford to hire a lawyer to seek enforcement in court, the consumer may not follow through with additional efforts to ensure that the policy is fully implemented. In small, homogeneous communities, if the entire community disagrees with a judicial policy, such as the prohibition on organized prayer in public schools, the judicial policy may be repeatedly violated but no consumers will be interested in pursuing actions to seek implementation of the public policy. Alternatively, consumers' resistance may defeat intended policies if they boycott schools to protest school desegregation or otherwise refuse to supply the public participation essential to the success of the public policy. Thus, consumers play an important role in the implementation, or lack thereof, of judicial policies.

Secondary Groups

There are many external political actors who influence the development and implementation of judicial decisions. The president and state governors are important enforcers of judicial policies. Their commitment, or lack thereof, to the enforcement of judicial decisions can significantly affect whether the judges' intentions are implemented. Interest groups frequently bear the burden of pressing for implementation of judicial decisions. Because the consumers who are supposed to be directly affected by the judicial policies frequently are not aware of court decisions or they lack the resources to seek enforcement of such decisions, interest groups utilize their organizational expertise and resources to initiate additional legal actions, publicize government officials' failure to obey judges' orders, lobby elected officials for enforcement, and otherwise seek to effectuate the judicial decisions that favor their policy preferences. The news media play an important role in disseminating information about judicial decisions so that interpreters, implementers, and consumers learn about recent policy directives. Moreover, the news reports help to keep the judges themselves informed about the consequences of their decisions and thereby influence future judicial decisions, including actions to accelerate implementation. Legislators, scholars, and others are also part of the judicial policy process through their actions, which influence and inform the actors most directly responsible for the interpretation and implementation of judges' decisions. Politicians may, for example, lend legitimacy and encouragement to citizens who resist judicial orders, as often occurred in school desegregation cases, and thereby hinder the effectuation of judicial policies.

The Consequences of the Implementation Process

Several scholarly studies provide examples of the effects of the implementation process in shaping, changing, and even negating judicial policy-making. For example, a study of lower court decisions concerning the public's right of access to judicial proceedings indicated that federal district court judges may resist implementation of Supreme Court decisions, even when there is no public opposition or significant controversy surrounding the judicial policy.[39]

Research on judicial policy-making indicates that the sources and quality of information available to implementers vary greatly from one city to another.[40] A study of police departments in Wisconsin in the aftermath of the *Miranda* decision found varying patterns of compliance with the Supreme Court's directive for police to inform criminal suspects of their rights.[41] The more professionalized departments received information about the decision from several sources, including formal conferences and training sessions.[42] Because the quality and completeness of information conveyed to police officers varied from department to department, the implementers in different cities had differing perceptions about the precise requirements of the judicial policy and its desirability. These mixed perceptions led to differing applications of the judicial policy depending upon the knowledge about and commitment to the policy possessed by the police officer making the arrest.

A study of compliance with Supreme Court decisions forbidding organized religious activities within public schools found that in one city "[w]hile superintendents soberly answered mail questionnaires to the effect that their schools were in full compliance with the Court's interpretation of the Constitution, many teachers led pupils in a wide variety of morning and afternoon prayers, Bible reading, and hymns."[43] In this community and other locales where the Supreme Court's policy directives were ignored, no implementer took responsibility for ensuring compliance. Moreover, school officials had little incentive to clash with the local consensus against the policy, especially when there were few consumers, if any, sufficiently interested and able to challenge the lack of compliance.[44]

As these examples demonstrate, judges are not omnipotent. The practical political world that they attempt to shape through their judicial policy-making is not readily controllable. Judges' decisions are influenced by the internal and external factors that guide judicial decision making. The consequences of judicial decisions are subsequently shaped by the degree of understanding and cooperation exhibited by the political actors who must implement court decrees. Without a high degree of cooperation and support from executive branch officials and the public, judicial policies may be rendered ineffective.[45]

Judicial Capacity

Serious concerns exist regarding the capacity of courts as policy-making forums. The nature of the judicial process creates risks that judicial policy outcomes will be based upon inadequate information and the assertion of narrow legal interests. In addition, the political forces that shape and hinder judicial outcomes in the implementation process undercut the purported effectiveness of courts. Although these issues are cause for concern, a complete assessment of policy-making processes in other branches of government casts doubt upon the proposition that courts are uniquely unqualified for policy-shaping activities. The quality of outcomes produced by courts will vary from court to court and case to case, depending upon the expectations and performance of individual judges and attorneys. Recognition of the flaws in judicial policy-making processes does not provide a basis for simple condemnation or support of courts' policy-making capacity. Observers should seek an understanding of the complexity of the policy-making processes in all branches of government *and* of the branches' interactions with each other in the policy process. Policy outcomes are not "good" or "bad" simply because they were shaped by a particular branch of government. Policy outcomes should be judged on their own merits with a recognition that all branches of government will continue to shape public policy and no branch of government is uniquely capable of developing "good" public policy for all issue areas.

CHAPTER 4
SCHOOL DESEGREGATION: FEDERAL JUDICIAL POWER AND SOCIAL CHANGE

RACIAL DISCRIMINATION HAS BEEN a continuing feature of American society since slave status became associated with skin color in the seventeenth century.[1] After the abolition of slavery in the mid-nineteenth century, the United States faced the consequences of its legacy of slavery. The prejudicial attitudes and discriminatory actions directed by the white majority toward African-Americans produced, among other things, discrimination in employment and housing, poverty, police brutality, and unequal access to public services. The harsh victimization of African-Americans clashed with the lofty ideals of "liberty" and "equal protection" that are trumpeted in the words of the U.S. Constitution. In systematically documenting the pervasiveness of racial prejudice and discrimination throughout American society in the 1930s and 1940s, Swedish sociologist Gunnar Myrdal captured the essence of the underlying contradiction between constitutional ideals and societal behavior with his aptly titled study, *An American Dilemma: The Negro and Modern Democracy.*[2]

For most of American history, African-Americans and their supporters gained little assistance from any governmental institutions in their efforts to seek fulfillment of the constitutional promise of "equal protection." In the aftermath of the Civil War, Congress passed several statutes aimed at combatting racial discrimination, but the nineteenth century justices on the U.S. Supreme Court nullified these legislative efforts. The Supreme Court declared in 1883 that because the Fourteenth Amendment says only that "No *State* shall . . . deny to any person . . . the equal protection of the laws" (emphasis supplied), Congress lacked the power to forbid discrimination by private individuals and businesses.[3] Subsequently, the Supreme Court endorsed official racial discrimination imposed by law in 1896 with the stipulation that the governmental treatment of different racial groups be "separate but equal."[4] Government at all levels, federal, state, and local, proceeded to enforce racial discrimination in employment, education, transportation, housing, and other spheres of American life, but no institution insured that the "equal" component of "separate but equal" policies was ever actually fulfilled. In fact, discriminatory policies produced decidedly unequal opportunities and services for African-Americans and other racial minority groups.

Viewed from the perspective of the 1990s, much has changed in American society with regard to racial discrimination. The focus of governmental policies changed in the second half of the twentieth century from the enforcement of racial discrimination to the official prohibition of it. The courts played a central role in the reversal of racial policies within the United States. Because of the success of lawyers in pursuing their claims in the courts, school desegregation litigation has served as the inspirational model for judicial policy-making initiatives concerning other civil rights issues. Advocates of women's rights, prison reform, and other causes emulated African-Americans' efforts to foster social change through judicial action. Acceptance of judicial declarations condemning racial discrimination is now so widespread in American society that "[a]nybody who opposed [such pronouncements] today would be assailed as a segregationist crank."[5] Despite general support for the judiciary's condemnation of racial discrimination, many questions remain concerning whether the courts have undertaken appropriate actions against discrimination and whether the consequences of judicial policy-making have helped or hindered the attainment of "equal protection" for all Americans.

The Litigation Strategy for School Desegregation

Before governmental institutions can undertake policy-shaping decisions, issues must be placed on their agendas. In the judicial context, issues are placed before the courts through litigation. Thus lawyers play a pivotal role in initiating judicial policy-making by pursuing cases and formulating arguments that will produce the desired responses from judges. Lawyers alone, however, cannot spark judicial action on policy issues. The judges who hear the cases must be receptive to the issues presented in order for litigation to produce judicial actions that shape public policy. Judicial action affecting school desegregation was the product of strategic litigation presented over several decades as the composition of the U.S. Supreme Court changed and became more receptive to arguments about the evils of racial discrimination.

Interest Group Litigation

The National Association for the Advancement of Colored People (NAACP) was founded in 1909 by prominent African-Americans and white liberals as an organization designed to employ political action in order to seek the eradication of racial discrimination. The NAACP lobbies legislative bodies, conducts voter registration drives, and engages in other activities designed to influence politics and public policy. In 1939, the NAACP created the Legal Defense Fund (LDF) as its component designed to pursue litigation in the courts. The LDF has been the primary advocacy organization in litigation concerning school desegregation, employment discrimination, capital punishment, and other issues both before and after the organization became independent from the NAACP in 1957.[6]

The NAACP's legal advisor during the 1930s was Charles H. Houston, an early African-American graduate of Harvard Law School. As dean of Howard University's Law School, he helped to educate a generation of African-American lawyers who used litigation to combat racial discrimination.[7] Houston's primary assistant at the NAACP and the first director of the LDF was Thurgood Marshall, one of Houston's former students and, eventually, the first African-American justice on the U.S. Supreme Court. Houston, Marshall, and the other NAACP-LDF attorneys were the primary architects of the litigation strategy that brought judicial attention to the problems of racial discrimination.

At the time that the NAACP began to attack discrimination through the courts in the 1930s, the law affecting racial segregation was clear and settled. The country was governed by the Supreme Court's 1896 decision that endorsed official segregation that was "separate but equal."[8] When a legal doctrine such as "separate but equal" is well-established and is the basis for federal, state, and local laws throughout the country, it can be difficult to persuade judges to undertake a dramatic reversal of pervasive, accepted social policy. Under the common law legal system that the United States inherited from Great Britain, judges are supposed to adhere to "case precedents" by following the decisions in previous legal cases. Although it is possible for precedents to be reversed if judges subsequently believe that prior cases were wrongly decided, usually case law changes gradually as judges make incremental modifications to precedents. In the 1930s, racial segregation was so firmly entrenched as an official policy and an accepted legal principle in American society that there was no reason to believe that courts would quickly undo the body of laws that made discriminatory practices pervasive throughout American society. Instead of directly challenging the constitutional basis for segregation, the NAACP and later LDF litigators initiated cases to show that "separate but equal" was a sham. In a series of cases that focused upon discrimination against African-Americans in graduate education at universities, the litigators attempted to show courts that there was plenty of "separate" but little or no "equal" in the segregated American education system.

Houston and Marshall sued on behalf of an African-American graduate of prestigious Amherst College who had been denied admission to the University of Maryland's Law School because of his race. Maryland's segregated university system had colleges for African-Americans, but the only law school was reserved for whites. In order to provide the appearance of "separate but equal," the Maryland legislature approved scholarships for African-American residents of Maryland to use in order to attend out-of-state law schools. However, the state never appropriated any money to actually pay for the scholarships that existed only on paper. The NAACP won a Maryland state court decision in 1936 ordering the admission of the African-American student to the University of Maryland's Law School because the state had failed to provide "equal" facilities under the "separate but equal" doctrine.[9]

Subsequent cases in the 1930s and 1940s brought before the U.S. Supreme Court the same issue concerning the absence of law schools for African-Americans in Missouri[10] and Oklahoma.[11] Like the Maryland court in the previous case, the U.S. Supreme Court recognized the lack of "equal" facilities for African-Americans and ordered the states to remedy this deficiency. States reacted by creating law schools for African-Americans, but the Supreme Court rejected these efforts in 1950 as still not "equal" after examining the newly-created separate law school in Texas (which consisted merely of three basement rooms in a state office building staffed by three part-time instructors).[12] A subsequent decision rejected the discriminatory practices in a graduate education program in Oklahoma in which the lone African-American student was forced to sit in a special "black seat" in each class, the library, and the cafeteria.[13]

The particular cases pursued by the NAACP reflected an incremental strategy aimed at chipping away the legitimacy of the "separate but equal" principle:

> Marshall's plan to act against the law school . . . made far more sense to Houston than frontal assault on the university. . . . The plan was to build a string of precedents, one victory leading to and supporting the next. The place to begin, Houston was convinced, was at the graduate-school level. And law schools were the most promising target of all, because judges were of course themselves lawyers who would be inclined to grasp the absurdity of a separate-but-equal law school for [African-Americans]. In a properly framed case brought in a moderate Southern state, no court would order the opening of a [black] law school or the closing down of a white one [as the means to achieve equality between the races].[14]

Thus there were several important elements to the incremental litigation strategy. By attacking law schools first, "separate but equal" could be exposed as a sham in a context which judges could understand. Judges and lawyers know better than anyone that, because established local law schools emphasize a particular state's laws, education at an out-of-state law school or at a hastily created, separate law school cannot provide equal education for people who intend to practice law in their home state. Moreover, desegregation among mature students in graduate schools was presumably less threatening to the white populace than the desegregation of grade schools, high schools, or colleges. Cases were initiated in "border" states, such as Maryland, Missouri, and Oklahoma, which had segregated systems but were more likely to have moderate judges and to have less virulently racist and violent political reactions to the gradual dismantling of segregation. Any cases initiated in the "Deep South," where segregation was more entrenched as a primary component of political ideology and daily life, were almost certain to produce adverse judicial decisions. Moreover, as the violence in Oxford, Mississippi in the 1960s subsequently demonstrated, any small inroads into segregation, such as registering one African-American student at the University of Mississippi, could lead to significant turmoil. President John Kennedy sent armed troops to enforce the desegregation of the University of Mississippi in 1962,[15] but it was unlikely that Presidents Franklin Roosevelt or Harry Truman would have taken such strong actions in the face of resistance to desegregation orders if the NAACP and LDF's initial strategy had directed litigation at the "Deep South" or at public school systems.

After the Supreme Court made favorable decisions concerning desegregation in higher education in 1950, the LDF launched its direct attack against the "separate but equal" doctrine in public schools. Lawsuits on behalf of African-American school children in several cities culminated in the Supreme Court's monumental opinion in *Brown v. Board of Education* that declared that 'in the field of public education the doctrine of 'separate but equal' has no place. Separate educational facilities are inherently unequal."[16] The LDF subsequently proceeded to file suits on behalf of African-American children in individual cities throughout the country during the 1960s and 1970s in order to seek the development and enforcement of desegregation plans for each segregated school system.

Litigation did not produce immediate changes in public policy. The NAACP began litigating discrimination issues concerning education in the early 1930s, but it was not until 1954 that the Supreme Court was prepared to declare that segregation violated the constitutional principle of "equal protection." It required many incremental judicial decisions to lay the groundwork for the establishment of a new precedent condemning official racial discrimination. Because of its glacial pace, litigation is not an especially effective strategy for public policy formulation *except*, as in the school desegregation cases, for circumstances in which the courts are the only branch of government receptive to arguments about the necessity of reshaping public policy concerning a particular issue. In such situations, judicial policy-making may be ineffective, but claimants have no other avenues for seeking policy changes.

Policy Advocates' Planning and Control of Litigation

Although the incremental strategy employed by the NAACP and LDF successfully moved the courts along a path toward the abolition of official segregation, it is difficult for interest groups to actually 'plan" litigation. As Stephen Wasby has noted:

> The received tradition about LDF's planned litigation would lead one to expect case selection to be governed by a highly developed set of regularly applied criteria. Instead, LDF was criticized by lawyers associated with it for not having done more to 'institutionalize" its process for deciding which cases to take and for not developing criteria for that purpose.[17]

Lawyers for interest groups cannot manufacture the ideal cases that they might wish to present to the courts. There must be an actual claimant whose victimization fits within the boundaries of recognizable legal claims. The claimant must be willing to pursue the case and to persevere through the hassles and delays of litigation. Thus the LDF and other interest groups that pursue policy issues through litigation must evaluate and accept cases on an *ad hoc* basis. Individual lawyers within the organization may disagree about which cases will provide the best vehicles for expending the interest group's limited resources.

In civil rights cases, interest groups' strategic litigation may be adversely affected by discrimination cases pursued independently by lawyers and claimants outside of the organization. These independent cases may be unsuccessful in advancing innovative arguments about discrimination and thereby inadvertently help to strengthen undesirable precedents. These undesirable judicial decisions then become additional obstacles for the interest groups' litigation goals.

Interest groups may also clash with each other by disagreeing about the best means to achieve the overriding goals of eradicating discrimination. For example, while the LDF sought complete desegregation of the Atlanta public schools, the Atlanta branch chapter of the NAACP accepted a compromise plan that limited the mixing of students but gave African-Americans greater control over the school through the hiring of African-Americans as school superintendent, administrators, and teachers.[18] Thus the focus of litigation can shift to a battle between interest groups that share a general goal but that disagree about the best means to attain the goal. In sum, interest groups, even when regarded as "successful" as in the school desegregation cases, lack the ability to plan and completely control litigation.

Judicial Remedies for School Segregation

When the justices of the Supreme Court considered drastically changing American social policy by declaring that school segregation violated the Constitution, they were very concerned about the possibility of adverse public reactions to their decision in *Brown v. Board of Education*. Chief Justice Earl Warren believed that such a drastic decision required unanimity among the justices.[19] Any majority on the Court could issue a decision with the authority of law, but only a unanimous decision would carry the full *force* of law by communicating to the entire nation that the highest court was united in its support for the new egalitarian policies. If the Court was divided over the issue of segregation, then opponents of change could justify their resistance to desegregation by saying, "See, even the justices cannot agree among themselves about what the law ought to be."

The Supreme Court's opinion in *Brown* was unanimous, but unanimity came at a price. Justice Stanley Reed, a Southerner from Kentucky, reluctantly became the final justice to agree to the decision outlawing racial segregation. However, in exchange for his reluctant agreement with the *Brown* opinion "he extracted from [Chief Justice] Warren . . . a pledge that the Court implementation decree would allow segregation to be dismantled gradually instead of being wrenched apart."[20]

The 1954 *Brown* opinion was a lofty and dramatic declaration that segregation of public schools violated the Equal Protection Clause of the Constitution. The justices did not, however, attempt to tell the nation how or when segregation would be dismantled. They deferred the issue of implementation until the following year.

In considering how to attempt to end the well-entrenched system of racial separation within American public schools, the Court had to be concerned about developing feasible mechanisms for change. The judiciary has little ability to enforce decrees on its own. It is dependent upon cooperation and acquiescence by the public. If there is overt resistance, the judiciary depends upon executive branch officials to carry out the judicial orders. Although President Dwight Eisenhower was not a strong supporter of civil rights and equality for African-Americans, the Eisenhower Administration's written arguments ("briefs") submitted to the Supreme Court in the *Brown* case had given the justices an indication that the Eisenhower Administration would provide some support for a decision against segregation. According to one of the government's attorneys at that time, the executive branch was "the first to suggest . . . that if the [Supreme] Court should hold that racial segregation in schools in unconstitutional, it should give district courts a reasonable period of time to work out the details and timing of implementation."[21]

In its 1955 *Brown* decision on the implementation question, the Supreme Court adopted the Eisenhower Administration's suggestion for gradual implementation by declaring that federal district judges should, on a case-by-case basis, develop and implement desegregation plans for individual cities "with all deliberate speed."[22] This gradual and ambiguous approach to implementation created opportunities for many school systems to resist and ignore the Supreme Court's decision that segregation violated the Constitution. The Court's acceptance of the need for gradual implementation eventually led to decades of litigation as people in communities throughout the country had to go to court again and again to seek fulfillment of the lofty principles enunciated in the first *Brown* decision. In retrospect, the Court's decision to move slowly against racial segregation led to undesirable delays in dismantling discrimination within public schools, yet the justices may have had no other alternative available to them:

> The Supreme Court's embrace of the "deliberate speed" formula is often criticized on the ground that it gave Southern states an excuse for avoiding compliance with the Court's ruling. But, according to [an attorney who worked for the Eisenhower Administration], the government would not have filed a brief without this formula, and the government's participation in the first [*Brown*] case was crucial, because it signaled to the Justices that the Executive Branch was ready to enforce a call for desegregation of public schools.[23]

Federal District Judges and Remedies for Segregation

Throughout American history, racial segregation in the public schools deprived African-American children of opportunities to receive equal educational opportunities. Elected officials, who are placed in office by and represent the majority of voters, frequently middle-class whites, never acted to redress the harmful victimization imposed upon African-Americans. Because no other branches of government were willing or able to act, civil rights advocates sought judicial assistance to change the detrimental policies of racial discrimination that were prevalent throughout the country. Twentieth-century litigation efforts by the NAACP coincided with favorable changes in the composition of the Supreme Court to lead to the Supreme Court's 1954 declaration that segregation violates the constitutional principle of equal protection. After announcing this general change in social policy, however, the Supreme Court passed the issue to the federal district courts for resolution. As one scholar has noted, "The decision in *Brown II* to remand cases to the trial courts for implementation of the constitutional principles declared in *Brown I* thrust the federal district judges into an unfamiliar and unwelcome position of prominence, and often notoriety, in their communities."[24]

The U.S. District Courts are the lowest level of courts in the federal judicial system. Unlike the Supreme Court, in which nine justices sit as a group to decide appellate cases together, the ninety-four district courts utilize individual judges presiding over their own trial courtrooms in which evidence is presented and initial findings and decisions are issued in legal cases. District judges possess no special expertise in regard to public education or any other areas of public policy. They are usually local lawyers who gained appointment to the federal bench through their connections, loyalty, and service to one of the political parties or to a United States senator.[25] Because they were unprepared and ill-equipped to "solve" the complex problem that had been placed in their laps, the district judges were generally cautious about forcing schools systems to change.

Critics of judicial intervention in segregated school systems often imply that federal judges exercised an opportunistic seizure of the public schools in order to advance their own ideological values. One critic, for example, has concluded that "[b]using . . . was foisted on a nation taken unaware by a small set of interlocking interest groups, judicial, academic, and bureaucratic idealists intoxicated by the rhetoric of governmentally managed social change."[26] It is true that civil rights advocates pushed for greater judicial intervention in order to undo the harms caused by decades of discrimination, but the image of a policy "captured" by a single interest group oversimplifies both the development and results of desegregation cases.

The Development of "Busing"

What was a district judge to do when confronted with evidence of racial discrimination in the public schools? Initially, judges often took the easiest course of action by declaring that individual school systems must end segregation and then permitting the schools to implement their own plans for ending discrimination. This preliminary stage of deference to local officials could be an eye-opening experience for many judges who were immediately confronted with both evasive actions by school officials and few visible changes in the segregated schools systems. For example, a detailed study of the desegregation case in the Charlotte, North Carolina public schools noted that the judge, who, like other district judges was a product of the local community in which his court was located, initially opposed the idea of school desegregation. The judge was a former president of the state bar association and was a prominent member of the local political establishment. According to the judge himself, as he heard evidence in the case and observed the resistance to change by local school officials, "reluctantly, but with increasing understanding, I listened and learned, and recorded what I learned."[27]

As in other cities, the judge in Charlotte initially permitted the district to implement a "freedom of choice" plan for student transfers between schools, which was the most common mechanism voluntarily adopted by school systems with segregated schools. Such plans could only foster change in the segregated schools to the extent that space was available for students to transfer into schools from which they were previously excluded. The potential for such plans to produce changes was also limited by the fact that African-American students transferring to previously all-white schools were subject to violence and harassment by whites. When the school officials who had maintained the segregated schools only reluctantly permitted transfers, there was little reason for transferring African-American students to expect institutional support in the face of threats and harassment. By 1964, ten years after the *Brown* decision, "freedom of choice" plans had created little change. Only 2 percent of African-American school children in eleven southern states attended desegregated schools.[28] The results in Charlotte were the same:

> A mere 2 percent of the black students in Charlotte—490 out of 20,000—were in schools with whites. More than 80 percent of the 490 were in one school with 7 white pupils; the remainder were distributed among 7 of the 103 schools in the school district. Virtually all blacks in Charlotte were still attending all-black schools.[29]

District judges' decisions are shaped and constrained by the decisions of the Supreme Court. The lack of change since 1954 and the obvious efforts of many school districts to avoid dismantling segregation led the Supreme Court to rethink its acceptance of "all deliberate speed" as the acceptable pace for desegregation. By 1969, the Supreme Court had declared that the "continued operation of segregated schools is no longer constitutionally permissible. Under the explicit holdings of this Court the obligation of every school district is to terminate dual systems at once."[30] This declaration accelerated the pace of innovation and intervention by district judges seeking to remedy the continuing problems that they observed in local school systems. In 1971, the judge in the Charlotte case imposed a busing plan on the school system, which was subsequently endorsed by the Supreme Court as an appropriate tool for ending segregated schools.[31] Thus, seventeen years after the *Brown* decision, the courts initiated the specific judicial policy mechanism, busing, that became the focus for many critics who claimed that courts had gone too far in dictating education policy.[32]

Again, it is useful to evaluate the issue of desegregation from the perspective of a judge. What should be done when there is evidence of the continuing existence of separate, inferior schools for African-American children? Should the judiciary merely announce that such results are improper and then leave it to the school officials to correct the problems? Is it, however, an abdication of the judicial responsibility for the protection of individuals' rights when those who caused the constitutional violations are permitted to develop—or to delay—their own remedies? Significant disagreements remain concerning the appropriate range of actions by judges in school desegregation cases. However, several observations are worth noting with regard to the implementation of this judicial policy. First, district judges did not seek responsibility for school desegregation cases. It was thrust upon them by the circumstances that led the Supreme Court to provide cautious, ambiguous directions for implementation of the *Brown* principles. Second, many districts were given the opportunity to develop their own plans for remedying segregation. However, because local officials were generally representatives of the people who benefitted from segregation, frequently there was little genuine effort to end the practices that so thoroughly disadvantaged African-Americans. Third, the most controversial and intrusive implementing mechanism, busing, which is highlighted by judicial critics as the symbol of improper judicial policy-making activities, did not gain widespread usage for more than a decade after the *Brown* decision. Judges turned to the use of busing after years of observing both resistance to desegregation and very few changes in segregated school systems. Thus, whether or not the policy of school desegregation is regarded as successful, the development of judicial actions to implement the policy are understandable as evolutionary reactions in the face of persistent resistance rather than as grand usurpations of power.

Assessing Judicial Policy-Making in School Desegregation

Limitations on Judicial Remedies

Busing as a means to achieve desegregation has been highly unpopular with the American public primarily because white parents do not want to send their children to schools in African-American neighborhoods. Politicians cultivated this opposition to increase their support among the white electorate. For example, "President Nixon did his best to exploit the [Democrats'] division [over busing] and to strengthen his antibusing credentials by repeatedly demanding congressional action to stop busing."[33] Although many politicians sought votes by assuring the public that the courts' busing orders would be thwarted, even Congressional efforts to countermand or limit judicial desegregation orders were never successful. The political turmoil generated by the public controversy over busing did, however, ultimately lead to a limitation upon judicial policy-making. This limitation came through the judiciary itself via its connections to the political system rather than through direct actions by other branches of government.

Because of several blunders by President Johnson in his efforts to appoint his confidante Justice Abe Fortas to replace retiring Chief Justice Earl Warren, President Nixon was able to appoint four justices to the Supreme Court during his first term in office.[34] Like any other president, Nixon sought to appoint justices who would share his political philosophy and values. Ultimately, the four Nixon appointees, joined by one holdover justice, comprised the narrow five to four majority in a 1974 decision that limited district judges' ability to design desegregation remedies.

A district judge had found evidence that the State of Michigan actively participated in creating and maintaining racial segregation in the Detroit public schools. Because the state, and not just the city, had been involved in creating the segregation, the judge required the state to share in implementing the remedy. In addition, because a high proportion of the Detroit school system's population was composed of African-American children, it was unlikely that desegregation could be achieved within the city limits alone. The judge's busing plan for correcting the problems of segregation ultimately required transporting students between the city of Detroit and fifty-three predominantly white suburbs.[35] The Supreme Court, increasingly composed of justices who were more conservative than their predecessors, narrowly declared that there could be no cross-district busing without clear proof of misconduct by suburban school districts.[36] Had the Supreme Court supported the mixing of city and suburban schools, there would have been a massive political backlash by affluent, middle-class suburbanites who enjoyed the benefits of superior school systems. In the words of several constitutional historians, "[r]eflecting the widespread opposition to busing among the general public, the Court . . . hesitated on the question of northern integration."[37]

The effect of the Supreme Court's decision was to limit district judges' options for developing desegregation plans. In the many major cities with large racial minority populations and deteriorating economic conditions, inner-city students were trapped in underfunded, inferior schools that were often within a few short miles of the very best schools in the country located in the nearby affluent suburbs. Because judicial remedies had to be confined within the boundaries of single school districts, judges could not develop remedies that would end the effective segregation of poor, minority students into inferior schools. As Donald Nieman observes about the Supreme Court's decision in the Detroit case, "[c]onsequently, the rapid progress toward school integration that had occurred during the late 1960s and early 1970s came to a halt; by the late 1980s, schools in most of the nation's large cities, where the majority of [African-Americans] lived, were more segregated than they had been in 1968."[38]

The Results of Judicial Desegregation Policies

There is a popular perception that judicial policy-making efforts to advance school desegregation have "failed." In the words of Lino Graglia, "the [Supreme] Court's decision to compel school racial integration is ineffective and self-defeating."[39] Indeed, there are obvious indications that the aspirations of *Brown v. Board of Education* remain unfulfilled. Minority children in major cities attend deteriorating schools that appear outwardly to be little different from the segregated schools that were targeted for elimination by the Supreme Court in the 1950s. In addition, the fear of busing has either maintained or accelerated the rate of "white flight" as middle-class people have increasingly departed from major cities' school systems.[40] This phenomenon has further contributed to the deterioration and segregated appearance of urban schools.

Despite these indicators of "failure," there have been many positive results of school desegregation that have been less noticed by the public. Desegregation plans that are implemented in the early grades can have positive effects upon minority students' academic achievement.[41] Even critics of desegregation can find no evidence that busing harms the academic achievement of white students.[42] Desegregation can also have positive effects upon students' attitudes toward people from other racial groups.[43] Although the news media often focused attention upon school systems in which there were protests, violence, or other problems, judicial desegregation orders have been accepted and "successful" in many other districts. As Gary Orfield has noted, for example, "[l]ittle attention has been paid to the small districts that serve about two-fifths of the nation's minority students. In many, the process of desegregation can be handled with little cost and few difficulties."[44]

Ironically, many of the larger cities that are regarded as "success stories" for judicial desegregation plans involve busing plans that cross city boundaries within county-wide school districts. These metropolitan desegregation plans that have been so successful are precisely the kinds of remedies that the Supreme Court precluded district judges from creating in its closely-divided decision concerning Detroit. Judges could only initiate such plans when a county-wide school system was already in existence. Only in such circumstances could a busing plan cross city lines while remaining within a single school district. The Supreme Court said that judges may not implement plans that cross district boundaries when school districts are separated by municipal boundaries, yet such metropolitan plans would be among the most effective desegregation programs as demonstrated by the relatively few cities that had independently developed county-wide school systems without a judicial order. County-wide, metropolitan districts decrease opportunities for "white flight," provide a large heterogenous student population to be mixed within the schools, and create incentives for everyone in the metropolitan area to work for the success of the desegregation program.[45] Thus, commentators cite cities with county-wide school systems, such as Charlotte, North Carolina and Tampa, Florida, as examples of successful desegregation programs.[46]

Judicial desegregation orders have produced both success and failure in attempting to reform public schools. By recognizing that the results of judicial desegregation orders vary depending upon the circumstances in which they are implemented, it becomes difficult to make any blanket assessment of judicial policy-making on this issue. In some cities, if judicial orders contributed to "white flight," then desegregation may have harmed school systems. After its composition changed during the Nixon era, the Supreme Court itself contributed to such adverse consequences by limiting remedial orders to individual city school systems and thereby inviting "white flight" from predominantly minority central city schools. The existence of adverse consequences does not mean, however, that judges should have done nothing. Because elected officials had created and maintained inferior schools for minority children, judges could not passively stand aside when presented with evidence of discriminatory acts. Judges felt understandably obligated to do *something*. Unfortunately, the actions that were available to them did not always lead to positive societal consequences.

In cases affecting many major cities, constraints were imposed upon district judges as the result of the political developments that changed the composition of the Supreme Court. These constraints made it impossible for judges to fashion effective desegregation plans for many cities. The failure of desegregation in large cities does not indicate that judicial policy-making in education will inevitably fail. It merely shows that, like other policymakers, the breadth of authority needed by judges for implementing effective policies can be limited by developments in the political system. Despite the protection of life tenure that insulates federal judges from direct political pressures, their policy-making activities are affected by the political developments that shape the composition, resources, and jurisdiction of the courts.

Like other policymakers, judges' success in developing and implementing judicial policies in education is influenced by the level of cooperation (or lack thereof) from the public and other political actors. The desegregation example demonstrates, however, that initial public opposition does not automatically defeat judicial policy initiatives. Public opposition manifested as "white flight" undercut judges' ability to implement busing plans, but general opposition alone did not prevent successful desegregation. Judges' orders to desegregate schools inevitably produced apprehension among different segments of the public about how changes in the schools would affect people's lives. In some cities, this apprehension manifested itself in violent opposition that produced the bombing of school buses, racially motivated attacks upon school children, and dynamite attacks against lawyers and judges.[47] Public opposition to desegregation does not necessarily prevent successful implementation because "protest demonstrations and protest voting are rare after the implementation year."[48] When people see and participate in desegregation plans that develop smoothly after the first year, they can come to accept the judicial policy.

In Charlotte, for example, opponents of desegregation, including mainstream community groups, ministers, and newspapers, organized protest marches against the district judge and extremists even firebombed the home, office, and car of the NAACP attorney who initiated the case.[49] A decade later, the success of the desegregation program led to a testimonial dinner by community leaders for the judge and the attorney as well as praise from the *New York Times*, the National Education Association, and other national observers.[50] Despite widespread opposition to the initial desegregation order in Charlotte, when the Supreme Court endorsed the district judge's busing plan, "[t]he community trauma began to be replaced by a desire to work out an orderly desegregation process acceptable to all but the extremists."[51]

The Symbolic Value of Judicial Policy-Making

Although there have been few improvements in the quality of education provided to poor, minority children in many major cities as a result of judicial policy-making in education, judicial action against segregation has arguably had broader effects upon society than merely those in the realm of education. The Supreme Court's decision in *Brown v. Board of Education* and subsequent decisions for nearly two decades conveyed a strong message to American society that racial discrimination was improper and should be abolished. All of the

73

Supreme Court's major decisions on school desegregation were unanimous from 1954 until 1973, when Nixon-appointee Justice William Rehnquist dissented in a case affecting Denver.[52] Thus, the Court put the full weight of its authority behind civil rights and equality in every major school desegregation case for nearly two decades.

In making consistent, strong, and authoritative statements against racial discrimination, the Supreme Court changed its role in regard to civil rights. For most of American history prior to the *Brown* decision, the Supreme Court had done relatively little to prevent racial discrimination. For example, the Court had provided judicial approval and legitimacy to the "separate but equal" doctrine that provided the underpinning for pervasive segregation and, as recently as the 1940s, the Court endorsed the incarceration of innocent Japanese-Americans in concentration camps during World War II.[53] Beginning with the *Brown* decision, however, on issues of racial equality the Supreme Court "serve[d] as a guide and even a pioneer in arriving at different standards of fair play and individual right" than those practiced at that time in American society.[54]

Although the Supreme Court's stated intention of ending segregation has yet to be fulfilled, the symbolic value of the Court's lofty language in *Brown* and consistent support for equality in subsequent cases helped to affect policy decisions by other political actors. The Court's decisions conferred legitimacy upon supporters of civil rights. As noted by Laurence Tribe, "*Brown v. Board of Education*'s mere declaration of rights profoundly affected the political dialogue in America. One reason was that this declaration of rights had in itself dramatically altered the country's perspective as to which group had law and order on its side."[55] By conferring legitimacy upon civil rights advocates, the Supreme Court "created hope for change and established rights to be vindicated by political action."[56] This, in turn, may have helped to encourage people to become politically active and thereby contributed to the mobilization of the civil rights movement. As one scholar observes, "[t]he development of the mass civil rights movement in the South probably was inevitable . . . [b]ut the Court may have speeded its growth."[57] Thus, "judicial decisions served more as mobilizing devices contributing to the broadening of American pluralism than as authoritative agents of change":[58]

> Although preferences were not changed by the law [pronounced by the Court], expectations were. . . . In the short term, the massive resistance to *Brown* and subsequent decisions overwhelmed the law. . . . But the ugly face of massive resistance, dramatized nightly on the television news, created a backlash among [Afri-

can-Americans], their supporters, and eventually the undecided. It was this backlash—among those whose hopes for integration were being frustrated and among formerly unengaged Americans who were angered by the failure to enforce Supreme Court decisions—that generated the civil rights movement and finally motivated the so-called political branches of government to support enforcement [of civil rights].[59]

The symbolic statements from the Court may have helped to set in motion other political developments that resulted in action by the president and Congress to enact civil rights laws: "Unable to pass a civil-rights act for seventy years, Congress enacted three in the decade after the *Brown* case."[60]

It is difficult to find specific evidence to document any unique or significant judicial impact upon social changes affecting equality. Although the judiciary's symbolic statements about equality endorsed the actions of civil rights activists, Gerald Rosenberg's thorough study of civil rights issues finds no empirical evidence from public opinion data or other sources to show that the courts *caused* significant social change.[61] Rosenberg argues that judicial actions to promote equality were simply one component of larger social forces moving American society and its political institutions toward a confrontation with discrimination.

As indicated by Rosenberg's study, apart from changes that occurred in specific cities, it is difficult to claim persuasively that judicial policy-making alone led to major social change. In fact, if the broader significance of judicial decision making on discrimination is primarily symbolic, then the judiciary's ultimate impact upon society may actually have hampered the attainment of equality. This is because the symbolic value of judicial policy declarations can also provide legitimacy for the persistence of inequality. Just as the *Brown* decision may have helped to raise expectations about equality and thereby motivate political action affecting other branches of government, the Supreme Court's reluctance to threaten suburbanites by tackling segregation problems in major cities may have conferred legitimacy upon the continued deprivation and isolation of poor, minority youngsters in inner cities:

> Even if it would have had no impact on judicial *remedies*, a judicial proclamation that inner city ghettoization was constitutionally infirm might have avoided legitimating this nationwide travesty [of severe segregation in large cities]. Had the Court exerted the one thing it clearly can control—its rights-declaration powers— . . . the Court could at least have created positive social and politi-

cal tension, the sort of tension that makes kids grow up thinking something is wrong, instead of inevitable, about ghettoization.[62]

The judiciary cannot always control the policy outcomes of the specific programs that it attempts to implement. It can, however, control the tone and content of the symbolic messages that it conveys to the American public.

Conclusion

Judicial policy-making concerning school desegregation is often regarded as the best example of the judiciary's role in fostering social change. Contrary to claims on behalf of effective judicial power, the popular belief that the Supreme Court rid the country of racial segregation does not withstand scrutiny. Judicial action helped to alter the practices of nearly all school systems and led to the successful desegregation of many school districts. However, political developments in American society (i.e., the election of President Nixon and his appointment of four new justices) affected the composition of the Supreme Court and thereby led to decisions limiting the judiciary's ability to plan and implement desegregation programs for large cities. The interest group litigation strategy that had been so successful in obtaining a favorable judicial declaration against segregation never achieved its ultimate goal of desegregated schools throughout the country.

Can judicial policy-making lead to social change? Perhaps—but not always in the manner in which the judges intended. The mixed record of success for school desegregation plans illustrates the weaknesses and limitations that beset judicial actions aimed at shaping education policies. Despite the continuing existence of inner-city schools that remain inferior and segregated in appearance, judicial policy-making had effects upon policy developments that extended beyond the successes and failures of desegregation in specific cities. The judiciary's strong, symbolic statements favoring equality may have assisted and sustained the mobilization of the civil rights movement that pressured the executive and legislative branches into finally enacting antidiscrimination statutes. Thus, the policy impact of judicial actions is intimately linked to the connections between the judiciary and the larger political system. The limitations upon judicial policy-making embodied in the Detroit case stemmed from developments in the political system that affected the composition of the Supreme Court. Similarly, any judicial influence over societal attitudes and legislative actions concerning civil rights flows from the impact of symbolic judicial pronouncements over the motivations and aspirations of interest groups and grassroots political movements.

CHAPTER 5
EDUCATION FINANCING:
JUDICIAL POLICY-MAKING IN
STATE COURTS

ACADEMIC RESEARCH ON JUDICIAL
policy-making usually focuses upon the federal court system with particular attention to the actions of the U.S. Supreme Court. The inordinate level of attention directed at the federal courts and the Supreme Court is understandable because of the federal judiciary's power over national policy controversies: "[T]he Supreme Court's policy-making is far more visible than the actions of most lower courts. . . . Because Supreme Court rulings potentially apply to the entire nation, they have far greater significance than those of most other courts."[1] Although the federal courts are the most prominent and well-known judicial policy-making forums, state judges are important policymakers, too.

Early legal cases established that the U.S. Supreme Court can review decisions from state court systems when those cases raise issues implicating federal law, usually in the form of questions about the meaning of the U.S. Constitution.[2] When state court cases raise issues exclusively concerning state statutes or provisions of state constitutions that do not involve federal law, then state courts are the authoritative decision makers. Thus, state courts can base decisions upon "independent and adequate state [law] grounds" in order to initiate innovative policies that the federal courts have declined to endorse nationwide.[3]

Litigants who seek to shape public policy through judicial decisions have two distinct options in pursuing court cases. If the federal courts are unreceptive to arguments about how judicial policies should be shaped, the arguments can be reformulated for presentation to state courts. Unlike federal court decisions, which can have a national impact, especially if pronounced by the Supreme Court, state court decisions only affect people within the borders of a single state. However, judicial policy decisions within one state may serve as examples for other state courts to emulate. The highest state courts in New York and California, for example, are famous for leading other states' courts to adopt innovations in tort law (i.e., personal injuries, negligence, etc.).[4]

The issue of education financing provides a good example of a policy issue that the federal courts declined to address but a few innovative state courts tackled with vigor. Over time, reformers in other states drew from the examples of the innovative state courts and increasingly utilized state court litigation as the means to seek education finance reform within their own states. As in the development of other judicial policies, state courts are components of their states' political systems and therefore find their decisions influenced by the actions of other actors and institutions.

Inequality in Funding for Education

Education is viewed as a cornerstone of democratic society: "In study after study social scientists have found a relatively high correlation between education and . . . political participation[,] . . . organization memberships, political knowledge, confidence, etc."[5] In the American democracy, with its ideological emphasis on equality of opportunity, the concept of equal educational opportunity "has been implicit in most educational practice throughout most of the period of public education in the nineteenth and twentieth centuries."[6] To achieve the goal of making public education available to all citizens, whether rich or poor, education financing mechanisms raised revenues by taxing the entire public rather than by making parents pay the full costs for their children's education. In an important 1874 court case in Michigan that helped to establish the principle of distributing the taxation burden for education throughout the public, famous jurist Thomas Cooley declared that education was "regarded as an important practical advantage to be supplied . . . to rich and poor alike, and not something . . . to be brought as such within the reach of those whose accumulated wealth enabled them to pay for it."[7] Thus, education was viewed as both a responsibility of government and as an essential building block for individuals' opportunities in American society.

Although public schools in every state provide education for children, the resources and hence the quality of education provided to students varies from city and city and from school to school. The most obvious disparities were those affecting African-American children, as discussed in chapter 4, that led to litigation and judicial decisions aimed at abolishing segregation in public schools. Racial discrimination was not, however, the only source of disparities in educational resources. Because public schools in the United States are divided into thousands of individual school districts, each governed by a separate board of education and school superintendent, there have always been significant differences in the administration of various school systems. Foremost among the differences is the fact that education funding within the United States has traditionally been based upon a property tax system. Thus each individual school system bears responsibility for raising its own revenues from the property owners within the district. Because there are great differences in the value of real estate from district to district and because some districts contain property owners more willing and able to pay higher tax rates, great disparities exist between districts with regard to the resources available for public education.

In Ohio in 1990, for example, a tiny district in which a major nuclear power plant was located reaped the benefits of having a large utility company paying taxes on highly valued property. Because of the substantial taxes paid by the power plant, this school district was able to spend $17,248 per pupil each year for the education of students within the district. By contrast, a poorer district in a rural county within the same state was able to spend only $2,900 per pupil each year for education because the district lacked taxable real estate with high property values.[8] Such disparities in financial resources can create great differences in the programs, supplies, class sizes, equipment, and other elements that affect the quality of education provided to students. Students in poorer districts are likely to receive inferior educational opportunities and their inferior schooling can affect their job prospects, incomes, and professional success for the rest of their lives.

During the 1930s and 1940s, several educators called attention to the unequal distribution of educational resources that affected the quality of schooling provided to America's children.[9] In 1940, the upper 10 percent of schools in the country spent more than $4,000 per classroom but the average spent in Mississippi was only $400 per classroom.[10] During the 1950s, states and the federal government greatly increased funding for education, partly in response to the perceived threat from the Soviet Union for supremacy in scientific and military affairs. During the 1960s, additional funds were directed toward poor inner-city school children to help remedy the great disadvantages created by years of discrimination against African-Americans. These efforts during both decades failed to redress the gross disparities that existed between school systems. Money from state and federal governments during the 1950s frequently went to rich districts as well as poor districts and did not balance unequal resources. Because of the substantial disparities in underlying property tax revenues, extra funds from government agencies did not close the resource gaps. In addition, money directed to poor students during the 1960s often was absorbed by ever-expanding school bureaucracies and therefore had limited impacts upon resource disparities affecting educational services delivered in inner-city classrooms.[11]

San Antonio Independent School District v. Rodriguez

Mexican-American parents in San Antonio, Texas initiated the major school financing case in 1968 that eventually arrived before the U.S. Supreme Court. As in other states, because Texas relied heavily upon property taxes to fund education, wealthy districts were able to generate significantly more money for their schools. The Edgewood Independent School District, located on the southwest side of San Antonio, taxed property at a rate of $1.05 per $100 of assessed value. This tax rate generated only $26 per pupil per year because the poor district did not contain valuable real estate. By contrast, the nearby Alamo Heights School District, located in an affluent suburban area, had a lower property tax rate of only $.85 per $100 of assessed property value, yet the district managed to raise $333 per pupil each year. In 1970, the average property value in Alamo Heights was $45,095 while in Edgewood it was only $5,429. Even if the parents in Edgewood sought to have their taxes raised in order to generate more resources, state laws in Texas prevented them from attaining the resources available in wealthy districts:

> Edgewood parents would have to tax themselves at twenty times the rate of those in Alamo Heights to match their revenues from property taxes. This would require a tax of almost $13 for each $100 of property value. But the state imposed a property tax ceiling of $1.50. ''The Texas system makes it impossible for poor districts to provide quality education,'' [the attorney for the Edgewood parents] concluded.[12]

The Texas state government's program for providing additional funds to schools exacerbated the resource gap between the Edgewood and Alamo Heights districts. The state provided an additional $225 per student to Alamo Heights, but only $222 per student in Edgewood. The federal government's aid to schools made a modest correction in the imbalance by providing $108 per student to Edgewood and only $26 per student to Alamo Heights. As a result of the funding formula, Alamo Heights could spend $238 more on each pupil than could Edgewood. This gap had obvious effects upon the educational resources provided to children in the two districts. For example, because Edgewood's teacher salaries were so low, almost half of its teachers did not qualify for state teaching certificates. They were merely college graduates who were given emergency certificates without any of the required training in education. By contrast, nearly 40 percent of the teachers in Alamo Heights had masters degrees. In addition, each school counselor in Edgewood had to help six times as many students as counselors did in Alamo Heights.[13]

The lawyers for the Edgewood parents argued that the education financing system violated the constitutional requirement in the Fourteenth Amendment that states not deprive people of the equal protection of the laws. They argued that the property tax system led to unequal treatment for school children who live in poor districts. The attorneys who defended the Texas system succeeded in persuading the federal judges in San Antonio to delay action on the case in order to permit the Texas legislature to reform the school financing system. The judges permitted the case to be delayed for three years, but they eventually took action when it became apparent that the Texas legislature was not going to address the issue of school financing. The district judges declared that the Texas financing system violated the equal protection requirements of the Constitution.[14]

Because judicial decisions are shaped by the attitudes, values, and policy preferences of the judges, the composition of an appellate court significantly influences the policy declarations produced by that court.[15] Thus, for example, Republican judges and Democratic judges tend to make different decisions concerning civil rights and civil liberties.[16] The decisions of the U.S. Supreme Court, like those in other appellate courts, are also shaped by these individualistic and political factors.[17] During his first term in office, President Richard Nixon had four opportunities to appoint new justices to the Supreme Court. He made his selections strategically in order to select jurists who would be reluctant to recognize and protect broadly claimants' assertions about violations of constitutional rights. Thus Nixon had tremendous influence over the composition of the Supreme Court at the time that the school financing case was decided. As a result, the four Nixon appointees, joined by one additional justice, comprised the five-member majority that rejected the Edgewood parents' claims.[18]

The five justices in the majority declared that there is no fundamental right to education and that economic status is not a protected classification under the Constitution's Equal Protection Clause. Although people are protected against racial discrimination by the Constitution, they are not protected against wealth discrimination. The majority claimed that any remedy for the harmful inequalities in education financing must come from elected officials in state legislatures, despite the fact that legislators, like others with political power in the United States, generally represent, and usually are themselves, affluent middle-class individuals who benefit from the disparities in school financing. Thus, Texas and other states could retain their school financing systems despite the adverse impacts upon students in poor districts.

In a famous dissenting opinion, Justice Thurgood Marshall complained that "the right of every American to an equal state in life, so far as the provision of a state service as important as education is concerned, is too vital to permit state discrimination."[19]

The Supreme Court's Reluctance to Act

The Supreme Court's reluctance to tackle the issue of education financing can be attributed to several sources. First, the Nixon appointees were philosophically disinclined to expand the protection of constitutional rights, especially in a decision that would clash with policies implemented by state legislatures. Second, the Supreme Court has historically been insensitive to the problems of wealth discrimination that produce adverse policy outcomes for poor people.[20] After studying Supreme Court cases, one scholar concluded that "[t]he decisions of the Supreme Court affecting the interests of the disadvantaged have evidenced an underenforcement of the equal protection principle."[21] Third, some members of the Supreme Court were probably very wary of the broad policy consequences and inevitable political backlash that would result from a decision favoring the Edgewood parents.

A decision against inequality would have required sweeping school finance reforms throughout the country. Individual districts' school boards would have lost their traditional control over local schools. Because Supreme Court decisions are not self-implementing, the justices may have feared that a major policy decision mandating reform would generate significant political opposition and resistance:

Two of the major contributions of the Warren Court to constitutional jurisprudence—the school desegregation and legislative apportionment decisions—required a willingness to devote extraordinary judicial resources to a continuing process of overseeing the responsive actions of other branches of government. In [San Antonio Independent School District v. Rodriguez] the Court may well have thought that attacking the school financing problem would have required just such an extraordinary devotion of resources; that prospect could have chilled the enthusiasm of a Court quite appalled by unequal educational financing.[22]

As Archibald Cox has noted, any decision favoring the Edgewood parents would have required the courts to force state and local governments either to spend more money or to redistribute the money available for education.[23] It is much easier for courts to order someone to stop doing something than it is for courts to make someone take specific actions. Thus, the Supreme Court shied away from facing the practical problems of implementing school financing reforms:

The difficulties have not always deterred the Court from placing affirmative duties on government . . . [as shown in school desegregation cases]; but it seems highly probable that the decisive factor . . . was the often practical difficulty of laying on communities essentially affirmative, on-going obligations for the benefit of disadvantaged groups.[24]

The Future of Supreme Court Policy-Making in Education

Critics of policy-making by courts regard judicial interference with government decisions on taxing and spending as the ultimate step in judicial activism that even the most ardent policymakers within the judiciary would never take. In Richard Morgan's words:

[H]ow long will it be before one of the "new breed" of federal judges nerve[s] himself up to the ultimate activism, ordering a state or municipality to raise taxes in order to upgrade some public facility or other to the level regarded by the Court as "minimally acceptable." But the business won't go that far. The shrewd activist judge will realize that such adventurism might expose the judicial branch to political retaliation of the sort bruted from time to time in Congress.[25]

Despite the Supreme Court's unwillingness to force state and local governments to spend money on the equalization of educational resources for students in poor districts, the justices do not always lack the will to challenge state and local governments in order to push for educational reform. In 1990, a five-member majority on the Supreme Court took the bold step of permitting a federal district judge to override a state law in order to push a local school district into raising taxes to pay for a school desegregation program.[26] Unlike their historical indifference to the education of poor people, several justices have had a long-standing interest in the issue of school desegregation. This interest may have provided them with sufficient motivation to initiate controversial policies.

Although the school desegregation decision demonstrated that the Supreme Court is not always deterred from risking public opposition to controversial policies, the Court's bold entry into the issue of taxation is likely to be a short-lived aberration. The five-member majority in the case contained three dissenters from the *San Antonio* case who rarely shied away from judicial policy-making in education, regardless of the potential controversy (William Brennan, Thurgood Marshall, Byron White), one justice who joined the Court after the *San Antonio* decision (John Paul Stevens), and a Nixon appointee who changed his judicial philosophy drastically in the years following his participation as a member of the *San Antonio* majority (Harry Blackmun). Because the majority was comprised of the five oldest justices on the Court, ranging in age from seventy to eighty-four at the time of the 1990 decision, for the foreseeable future this case may represent the "last hurrah" for controversial Supreme Court policy-making affecting educational administration. The dissenters in the case, Chief Justice William Rehnquist and the three younger, more conservative Reagan appointees (Anthony Kennedy, Antonin Scalia, Sandra Day O'Connor), were obviously eager to overturn this precedent. With the retirements of Justice Brennan at the end of the Court's 1989–1990 term and Justice Marshall in 1991, the balance shifted in favor of those justices who oppose judicial policy-making in educational administration, even in desegregation cases.

State Courts and Education Finance Reform

During the 1970s, because the Nixon appointees to the Supreme Court slowed efforts to expand and protect individuals' constitutional rights through judicial policy decisions, commentators, including Justice William Brennan, began to discuss the possibilities for utilizing state constitutions as a basis for judicial policy-making.[27] The constitutions of many states contain more specific protections for the rights of individuals than do the provisions of the U.S. Constitution. For example, some state constitutions contain specific rights concerning privacy, gender equality, and environmental quality that are not explicitly contained in the federal constitution.[28] In addition, as the U.S. Supreme Court does in regard to the federal constitution, state supreme courts have the opportunity to apply their authority for interpreting state constitutions and statutes in order to identify new rights and develop policies favored by the judges. As with the federal courts, the state judges' inclination to engage in policy-making may depend upon their attitudes, values, and policy preferences.

One key difference between state and federal courts looms as a significant potential influence over judicial policy-making. Because of the manner in which they are selected, judges in many state court systems face a specific deterrent not faced by federal judges that may discourage their judicial policy-making decisions. Federal judges enjoy life tenure. They serve "during good Behavior" unless they are impeached for violating criminal laws or for otherwise engaging in gross ethical improprieties. This protected tenure is designed to insulate federal judges from political pressures and enable them to make courageous and potentially unpopular decisions. By contrast, judges in most states run for election, and even judges in the states that employ merit selection appointments must face periodic retention elections.[29] Thus many state judges, unlike federal judges, risk the possibility of removal from office if the public disagrees with controversial policy-making decisions. Despite their potential vulnerability, state judges have increasingly filled the void left by the Supreme Court's unwillingness to tackle the issue of education finance reform.

Early Reform Cases in State Courts

In two states, claimants seeking to reform school financing systems actually gained favorable decisions from state courts prior to the Supreme Court's decision in the *San Antonio* case. The use of litigation to seek reform was spurred by the California Supreme Court's 1971 decision in *Serrano v. Priest*, which declared that equal protection guarantees in the California constitution invalidated the property tax system that led to unequal financing for California schools.[30] The *Serrano* decision prompted a flurry of lawsuits in various states seeking school finance reform. Attorneys representing parents and students in poor districts elsewhere hoped that courts in other states would use the California Supreme Court's example to find that property tax systems and their resulting inequities were unlawful. Unfortunately for these litigants seeking to utilize judicial policy-making to their advantage, the U.S. Supreme Court's 1973 decision in the *San Antonio* case seemed to persuade state courts to avoid judicial involvement in school finance issues.[31]

In a second case initiated before the Supreme Court's 1973 decision, the justices on the New Jersey Supreme Court declared their state's school financing system to be unconstitutional.[32] As the basis for its decision, the court interpreted a specific provision within the New Jersey Constitution that required "a thorough and efficient system of free public schools."[33] Although nearly all state constitutions contain provisions concerning free public education, courts in other states were less willing to employ their interpretive powers in order to intervene in educational administration. Thus the New Jersey decision did not immediately serve as the basis for many successful lawsuits elsewhere. From 1977 to 1983, courts in five additional states recognized a right to equality in education but courts in fifteen other states rejected such claims based upon state constitutions.[34]

Later Reform Cases

By the late 1980s, the issue of educational quality in American schools had risen on the nation's policy agenda to become an issue of importance to public officials and society at large. Because of unfavorable comparisons between American schools and those in other industrialized countries and because the United States was losing its place as the world's dominant economic power, Americans became convinced that public education must be improved in order for the country to remain successful in an increasingly competitive world economy. Coinciding with the greater societal interest in education issues was an increasing willingness of judges in some states to tackle the issue of school finance.

In 1984, superintendents in Kentucky's poorer school districts banded together to challenge inequities in the state's system for financing public education. Initially, leaders in the state's legislature asked the superintendents to wait until the legislature had the opportunity to develop reforms, but legislative inaction led to a lawsuit on behalf of sixty-six districts in 1985. Because litigation is characteristically a slow process through which to seek policy change, the trial in the case did not take place until late 1987 and early 1988.[35] In 1988, a state trial judge ruled that the state's financing system violated the Kentucky Constitution by providing inferior educational opportunities to children in poorer school districts.[36] The Kentucky Supreme Court upheld this decision in 1989 and the governor and state legislature subsequently acted quickly to overhaul the state's educational system in 1990.

In Texas, the disparities between school districts continued to grow after the U.S. Supreme Court declined to take action in the 1973 *San Antonio* case. By 1988, the $238-per-pupil disparity between Edgewood and Alamo Heights had grown to a whopping $1,300 per pupil per year.[37] In 1989, when the disparity between Edgewood and the wealthiest districts in the state had reached as much as $8,400 per pupil per year, the Texas Supreme Court intervened and declared that the financing system violated the Texas Constitution.[38] Eighteen months later, the Texas legislature finally enacted an education finance reform law that gained the approval of the state judge who originally found the system to be unconstitutional.[39]

The cases in Kentucky and Texas are the two most prominent examples of an accelerating trend toward seeking state judicial policy-making in the absence of action by state legislatures or the U.S. Supreme Court. In the late 1980s, lawsuits were initiated in nearly two dozen states to seek reform in education financing.[40] The U.S. Supreme Court could have forced the equalization issue upon state governments nationwide in the *San Antonio* case in 1973, but it declined to do so. The inaction by the nation's highest court did not, however, end the policy controversy. Nearly two decades later, the policy changes avoided by the Supreme Court were tackled on a state-by-state basis by judges in state court systems. The political interests seeking reform employed patience and persistence to find the opportune moment (i.e., the late 1980s) and the interested policymaker (i.e., state judges) necessary for successfully developing policy changes.

The Consequences of State Judicial Policy-Making

As with other public policy issues addressed by the courts, successful reform of education financing systems could not be controlled by state judges. Judges can issue policy declarations and threaten legal sanctions (e.g., contempt of court citations, injunctions, etc.) against recalcitrant government officials, but the judges cannot single-handedly insure that policy changes actually occur. State judges, like federal judges, are dependent upon the cooperation and acquiescence of government officials and the public. Thus policy-making activities by state courts involve complex interactions between a variety of interested political actors within a state.

California

In California, the judicial decisions ordering the implementation of reforms did not lead to quick or easy remedies for funding inequalities. One scholar who studied the implementation of the California Supreme Court's decision concluded that the court "serve[d] as a catalyst to change rather than as a formulator of precise policy"[41] and that "The court in *Serrano* appeared to be less concerned with specifying a precise system of financing that should be implemented than it was with moving the legislature toward developing a new system that would be less tied to the wealth of the district."[42]

The California legislature acted to develop a gradual program to reduce disparities, but the implementation process became complicated by the California taxpayers' revolt of the late 1970s. By passing the Proposition 13 referendum in 1978 to limit property taxes, the taxpayers passed greater responsibility for education funding from the local districts to the state and thereby created an opportunity for the state government to equalize education funding.[43] However, the state legislature bowed to the political power of wealthier districts and instituted a plan that actually sent more money to wealthier districts than to poorer districts as part of a program to implement gradual reductions in resource disparities.[44] Although reformers won a victory with the California Supreme Court's judicial policy declaration, the timing and success of intended reforms were thwarted because policy implementation depends upon political actors and institutions, such as governors and legislatures, that cannot be readily controlled by judges.

Texas

In Texas, the unsuccessful litigation in the 1973 *San Antonio* case produced some modest legislative activity in regard to education finance reform. A study comparing the policy consequences for the successful court cases in California and New Jersey with the unsuccessful initial case in Texas found that all of the cases had similar results: modest changes. Thus, in some important respects, the function of judicial policy-making is not always to dictate precise policies to society; it frequently performs a legislative agenda-setting function by drawing elected officials' attention to a particular policy problem.[45] Thus unsuccessful lawsuits and even the mere threat of litigation may create policy consequences similar to those in "winning" cases if the litigation process serves to spur other political actors to take action on a particular public policy issue.

Obviously, the subsequent state court litigation in Texas indicated that the modest reforms in the aftermath of *San Antonio* had only limited effects upon harmful resource disparities. The decision by the Texas Supreme Court in 1989 was similar to that of the California Supreme Court in that the judicial action did not provide specific instructions to the legislature. By issuing a unanimous decision, the Texas court attempted to place its full authoritative legitimacy behind an effort to push the state legislature into action:

> Texas Supreme Court justices are elected officials, and the Court is composed of both liberals and conservatives, Democrats and Republicans. The desire for unanimity no doubt arose from a belief that the decision was as much a political statement of the necessity for school finance reform as it was a constitutional interpretation. Therefore, bipartisan consent was a major objective of the generalized opinion. The Court apparently viewed itself as a "catalyst for change" as opposed to a provider of strict constitutional guidance.[46]

The Texas legislature was unable to agree upon a plan for equalizing educational resources. Any specific proposal threatened the status of particular political interests, including wealthier districts, teachers, and taxpayers, so the legislature had trouble finding a formula that could generate sufficient consensus for enactment. Resistance to judicial policy-making was quite evident. The governor proposed an amendment to the state constitution that would declare that education was *not* a constitutional right in order to erase the basis for the state judges' decisions on school financing. The legislature stalled its efforts to develop reforms in the hope that the state supreme court would eventually overturn lower court decisions mandating changes.[47] Ultimately, with persistent pressure from a unified state judiciary and the election of a new governor who was more sympathetic to reform, the legislature enacted an equalization law that was satisfactory to the presiding judge. It took four special legislative sessions and a judicial threat to halt state-aid payments to public schools before the bill was finally passed. Despite the apparent resolution of the policy battle that lasted over two decades, lawyers representing poorer districts and those representing wealthier districts examined the new law with an eye toward further legal challenges if they found the consequences of the equalization statute to be unsatisfactory to their respective interests.[48] Judicial policy issues do not necessarily become resolved because there are always opportunities for further challenges and changes, especially, as chapter 7 will discuss in regard to abortion, when the composition of the judiciary changes.

Other States

Every state in which courts attempted to force reform of education financing policies experienced continuing political battles over the form and implementation of the new policies. In New Jersey, the state supreme court had to issue seven separate decisions from 1973 to 1976 as it pushed the state legislature to both design and fund an equalization program.[49] The development of reforms did not solve the problems of inequalities in school financing because twelve years later in 1988, a New Jersey judge once again ruled that the state's school financing law did not comply with the state constitution.[50] Policy battles can continue long after the initial judicial "resolution."

In Kentucky, the entire state seemed to rally behind the effort to reform the education system. One year after the state supreme court upheld the lower court decision declaring the funding system invalid, the legislature and governor enacted a comprehensive reform bill. Despite increases in taxes as a component of the legislation, the comprehensive educational reform effort appeared to have the support of the public.[51] Politicians seeking higher elective offices positioned themselves to exploit the expected taxpayer backlash that did not immediately emerge. As long as the public appeared to support the education reforms, the political candidates had praise for the reforms. However, some candidates began to drop hints of dissatisfaction with the increased taxes in anticipation of later taxpayer unhappiness. Ironically, the candidate for lieutenant governor who tried to make an issue of the tax increases included in the reform package was the very same former trial court judge who originally ruled that the state's financing system was unconstitutional.[52] His decisions initiated the process of reform but then he subsequently implied that the reforms had gone too far—although his comments were motivated, at least in part, by his desire to win election to office. His shift between the judiciary and the electoral political arena was a stark reminder of the intimate and enduring connections between courts and partisan politics which shape continuing developments as judicial policies are initiated, implemented, and, sometimes, discarded.

Conclusion

Although scholars and the news media give inordinate attention to the policy-making activities of the U.S. Supreme Court and the other federal courts, state judges must also be recognized as important, influential policymakers. Reformers who utilize litigation to attain desired policy outcomes frequently avoid state judges because of a perception that these elected officials cannot make independent decisions due to their intimate connections to local political interests and their need to please the voters. This point is well-illustrated in a book describing the collapse of a coal company's dam and the subsequent lawsuit on behalf of people injured in the ensuing flood. Because of fears that the local lawyers and judges were too friendly with the powerful owners of the coal company, the attorneys for the injured people did everything in their power to have the case moved to federal court.[53] In the case of school finance litigation, however, the U.S. Supreme Court indicated very clearly in the *San Antonio* case that the federal courts would not intervene in this policy issue. Without access to the federal courts, reformers seeking policy changes must consider the other forums available to them. Because legislatures created and maintained the financing systems that claimants wished to challenge, state courts emerged as virtually the only policy-making forum that presented any possibility for successful authoritative declarations favoring reform.

Although state constitutions provide a basis for judicial policy decisions by state judges on education finance reform, relatively few state courts have acted on this policy issue. A few innovative courts led the way with decisions in the 1970s, but other state courts followed the lead of the U.S. Supreme Court by declining to become involved in the issue of unequal educational resources. After the issue was presented unsuccessfully to legislatures for several decades and national economic problems led to heightened public interest in education issues, more state courts became willing to take action on disparities in education financing. Further activity by state courts will serve to encourage litigants in additional states to initiate lawsuits in the hope that their state judiciaries will emulate the recent trend.[54]

As in other examples of judicial policy-making, state courts possess a limited ability to implement policy changes effectively. They are dependent upon cooperation and compliance from government officials and the public. Thus, state judges frequently function merely to force policy issues upon the agendas of state legislatures while the judges simultaneously attempt to apply consistent pressure on elected officials to take remedial actions. The process of judicial policy-making can be slow and ineffective unless, as in Kentucky, the judges' policy interests coincide with those of the elected officials who must design and implement reforms.

CHAPTER 6
PRISON REFORM LITIGATION: JUDICIAL POWER AND INSTITUTIONAL ADMINISTRATION

JUDICIAL INTERVENTION INTO THE affairs of correctional institutions is one of the most controversial aspects of policy-making activities by courts. In their efforts to force correctional administrators to meet constitutional standards for prison conditions and treatment of inmates, several judges have eventually placed themselves in charge of the day-to-day operations of prisons. There is no question that the management of correctional institutions is normally regarded as an executive branch function. If, however, government officials fail to comply with judicial orders concerning the conditions in prisons, does the administration of prisons properly become a component of the courts' policy-making role as judges seek to ensure that policies are actually implemented? Obviously, judicial control over the daily management of decisions within an executive branch agency heightens the concerns that judges have gone too far in imposing their policy preferences upon society.

Courts and Prison Administration: Historical Background

Traditionally, courts took a "hands off" approach when prisoners requested judicial protection from harsh treatment by correctional administrators. When prisoners filed claims in court to seek protection of asserted rights, judges responded by declaring either that prisoners were "slaves" of the state and therefore possessed no rights[1] or that judges must defer to the decisions of prison officials who are society's experts on correctional administration.[2] Judicial intervention into prisons did not begin until the 1960s, an era in which American courts became more receptive to claims from political minorities seeking judicial protection of constitutional rights. The success of African-Americans' civil rights movement precipitated the formation of legal assistance organizations and the assertion of constitutional claims on behalf of members of a variety of powerless groups, including mental patients, welfare recipients, physically handicapped people, and convicted criminal offenders. Other groups attempted to emulate racial minority groups' success in seeking judicial assistance for the definition and protection of constitutional rights.

Prisoners achieved a major legal breakthrough when the Supreme Court decided in 1964 that prisoners could utilize a federal statute as the basis for lawsuits to challenge the conditions of their confinement.[3] As a result, prisoners file suits under Section 1983 of Title 42 in the United States Code, a statute that permits suits against state officials to be filed in federal courts, in order to assert claims of constitutional rights violations.

Courts were called upon to evaluate claims asserting violations of a variety of constitutional rights. Prison officials vigorously resisted any judicial supervision of correctional institutions. Such resistance was a natural response to external threats against their authority, their autonomy, and the existing order within institutions. In most successful cases concerning constitutional rights of prisoners, judges' decisions lead to modest changes in prison policies. For example, judges have enforced First Amendment religious rights of prisoners by ordering that Muslim prisoners be permitted to pray, to have access to their religious literature, and otherwise to practice their religious beliefs as long as those practices do not threaten institutional security.[4] Because claims concerning most constitutional protections, such as Fourth Amendment search and seizure rights, First Amendment free expression rights, and Fourteenth Amendment procedural due process rights, have been strictly limited as courts emphasize institutional order and security as the primary policy goal, many court decisions do not drastically change existing prison practices. In regard to the Eighth Amendment's prohibition on cruel and unusual punishments, however, judicial intervention has had tremendous impact upon correctional administration because Eighth Amendment claims serve as the basis for judges' evaluations concerning whether living conditions within prisons meet constitutional standards.

When judges began to evaluate claims about inhuman conditions within prisons, they sometimes discovered state-sanctioned brutality and living conditions that were labeled unfit for human habitation by public health officials. In Arkansas, for example, prisoners were tortured with electric shocks and denied access to medical care. In addition, corrections officers remained outside the cellblocks and permitted "trusty" inmates to maintain order by administering brutal beatings upon other inmates.[5] One scholar described the conditions in Alabama's prisons:

> In 1976, the prisons were "unfit for human habitation." They were filthy, noisy, dimly lit, unventilated, vermin-infested affronts to decency. Prisoners were denied the most basic means of personal hygiene—toothbrushes, toothpaste, shaving cream. Food was prepared in grossly unsanitary conditions, with neither the supervision of trained professionals nor occasional checks by public health officials.[6]

With varying degrees of severity, other correctional institutions had similar problems concerning violence, overcrowding, adequate sanitation, medical care, and other aspects of prison living conditions. By the late 1980s, virtually every state had local jails or state prisons that had been forced to modify facilities or procedures as the result of court orders.

The Propriety of Judicial Intervention

Should the courts intervene on behalf of prisoners? Many people believe that criminal offenders should forfeit the legal protections of citizenship because they have caused harm to society. The U.S. Constitution, however, provides no exclusion for lawbreakers. Indeed, the Eighth Amendment's prohibition on cruel and unusual punishments clearly implies a limitation upon what the government can do to criminals. If courts returned to the "hands off" policy and thus there were no constitutional protections enforced on behalf of prisoners, questions would arise once again concerning American society's commitment to legal rules and to humane treatment of prisoners. Many examples are available of troubling situations that would collide with the purported commitment to individual rights within the United States. Should someone arrested but not yet convicted—and therefore "presumed innocent"—of a minor offense be effectively subjected to the death penalty because local jail officials never developed a plan for removing prisoners in the event of a fire? Should someone convicted of a minor offense be effectively subjected to the death penalty by being deprived of food, water, or medical care? The examples could go on and on.

The impetus for judicial intervention into prisons stems from several factors. Obviously, the judicial responsibility for enforcing constitutional rights makes it difficult for contemporary judges to defer completely to correctional administrators and thereby ignore actions that inflict unconscionable harm upon individuals who depend upon state officials for food, water, housing, medical care, and the other essential elements of human survival. In addition, Americans' perceptions of a mushrooming problem with crime in American society have led elected officials to seize upon crime as a useful issue for gaining political support.[7] Politicians catered to the voters' desires in the 1970s and 1980s by continually increasing the severity of punishments mandated for various crimes. The increasing severity in punishments led to tremendous increases in the American prison population, from 196,429 prisoners in 1970[8] to 710,054 in 1989,[9] but legislators did not provide corresponding increases in resources for corrections. Taxpayers and politicians want to punish criminal offenders severely, but they do not want to expend state revenues upon corrections systems. The increasing inmate populations and limited resources place correctional institutions under extreme pressures and lead to problems in maintaining both internal security and adequate living conditions. Because other branches of government created these conditions in response to demands from the public, only the judiciary is available to push the legislative and executive branches to expend the necessary resources in order to maintain constitutional standards within correctional institutions. Supporters and opponents of courts' role in shaping correctional policies can generally agree that *sometimes* it is necessary for judges to intervene into the affairs of prisons. There is great disagreement, however, about when such intervention is appropriate and about how involved judges should become in dictating policies and managing programs in correctional institutions.

The Initiation of Judicial Intervention

Judicial intervention into prisons is initiated through the filing of a complaint by one or more prisoners alleging constitutional violations by state officials who administer prisons. Complaints filed by prisoners in federal courts frequently list many complaints against the institution, most of which provide no basis for a proper legal action grounded in an asserted violation of the U.S. Constitution. In prisoner litigation, three differet types of actors may undertake the "legalization process" for translating prisoners' grievances into issues that courts may consider. First, prisoners themselves may be able to identify and present constitutional issues regarding the Eighth or other Amendments that provide a basis for judicial examination of prison policies. Because indigent prisoners have no right to receive free assistance from attorneys in civil rights actions, they must often attempt to represent themselves. Litigants, including prisoners, who represent themselves in court are known as "*pro se* litigants." Although most prisoners lack the skills to utilize the prison law libraries that have been provided to prisoners pursuant to a Supreme Court decision guaranteeing that prisoners have access to the courts,[10] a few self-trained "jailhouse lawyers" have developed sufficient knowledge and skills in litigation to present effective claims. Second, interest groups, such as the American Civil Liberties Union's National Prison Project or the Legal Defense Fund, may initiate litigation on behalf of prisoners in order to seek judicial reform of correctional institutions. Third, personnel within the federal court itself may undertake the "legalization process" of transforming lay prisoners' complaints into recognizable constitutional claims. Some federal district courts have "*pro se* law clerks," usually inexperienced attorneys whose job focuses upon sifting through *pro se* petitions from prisoners in order to determine if any recognizable constitutional claims lurk beneath the often disjointed, semi-literate complaints.[11] In other federal courts, the law clerks who work directly under a specific judge will handle *pro se* petitions along with their many other responsibilities.

Because so few prisoners are capable of effectively presenting claims, there is great dependence upon outsiders to transform complaints into proper legal form. Interest groups that assist prisoners have relatively few resources and therefore must be very selective about which cases they wish to pursue. Interest groups strategically select a small number of cases that embody prison reform issues of broad interest so that a favorable decision in a chosen case may lead to reforms in more than one institution. Thus interest groups may avoid complaints concerning problems that are specific to one institution— unless the conditions at that institution are particularly objectionable. Although the process of legalizing complaints in order to transform them into a proper form inevitably narrows the courts' focus, interest groups may consciously attempt to provide courts with a broader focus in order to influence litigation and reforms across the country.

It may seem odd that actors within the federal courts participate in the transformation process on behalf of *pro se* litigants, but the federal judiciary has made a commitment to accommodate complainants who cannot afford professional legal assistance. The substance of the actual assistance provided to prisoner-litigants by law clerks may not match the symbolic implications of providing personnel to review prisoners' petitions carefully. Research on prisoners' petitions has raised questions about how thoroughly and carefully law clerks actually review such claims. One study of more than 4,500 prisoners' civil rights petitions found that "virtually all of the inmates' cases are dismissed," with fewer than 7 percent reaching the trial stage.[12] Although there is disagreement about whether the high dismissal rate indicates bias against prisoners' claims[13] or the lack of substance in most petitions,[14] there are genuine risks that the continuing burden of these routine cases upon federal court personnel creates incentives to seek reasons to dismiss such cases rather than to look carefully for meritorious claims:

> In regard to prisoners' cases, there was a perceptible risk that [judicial officers] and their law clerks, who are accustomed to dismissing such cases, approach the case files by first asking, "How can I dismiss this case?" rather than asking, "Does this case have any merit?" The [judicial officers] have an interest in seeing prisoners' cases dismissed, not simply for their functional role as gatekeepers and filterers, but in a personal sense, because it permits them to avoid holding conferences and hearings with a class of potentially difficult and hostile litigants.[15]

Thus it is doubtful that many judicial officers are actively seeking opportunities to intervene into correctional institutions. Most prisoner claims are never considered by the federal courts because of the dependence upon self-interested outsiders for selectively transforming complaints into legal issues.

If a judge identifies significant constitutional issues underlying a prisoner's complaint, the court may appoint attorneys to prepare and present the case on behalf of the prisoner. In the controversial judicial intervention into the Texas Department of Corrections, the judge "appointed a few of the country's leading prison litigation attorneys to represent inmates and brought in the United States Department of Justice as an adversary to the State of Texas."[16] Not surprisingly, when litigation is carried forward by interest groups or by reform-oriented attorneys appointed by the court, the case can soon leave the actual prisoner-plaintiffs forgotten in the background. In effect, a second level of transformation may occur. Not only is the original complaint "legalized" to raise issues for the court, the subsequent litigation may be transformed to examine the policies of the prison system generally instead of the specific complaints of the prisoners who initiated the action. In litigation that reformed the Georgia State Prison, the original plaintiffs were forgotten as the litigation moved forward:

> The lack of even one key decision-making plaintiff inmate directly affected by the changes from *Guthrie* [*v. Evans*] dramatically illustrates how the polycentric institutional reform case differs from ordinary civil litigation. In ordinary civil litigation, cases depend on the decisions of the parties, especially the plaintiff. Yet the plaintiff inmates in *Guthrie* were sometimes so invisible to the key decision makers that they complained for three years that they were not even informed of the progress on their own case.[17]

The judge plays an important role in determining the breadth of the examination of the corrections policy through appointment of counsel and the definition of relevant issues. In the Texas case, for example, the judge "instituted a procedure whereby issues not raised by the inmate plaintiffs—crowding, recreational facilities, prison land use, and many others—came under his review."[18] Although this broadening process may lose sight of the normal goal of judicial responsiveness to individual claimants, the second level transformation process may diminish concerns that judicial policy-making focuses too narrowly upon only the interests of selected, unrepresentative plaintiffs.

Processing Prison Litigation

Structured Negotiation

The litigation process in prison reform litigation does not generally resemble the stereotypical adversarial process. Although state and local governments generally fight against prison reform litigation, their efforts frequently serve, in effect, to control the costs of reforms that might be imposed upon them and to provide a basis for their participation in shaping the reforms that will redress persistent problems. Thus much of the action in prison reform litigation involves negotiation within the structured environment of federal court procedures. In the Georgia case, for example, the judge ordered the contending parties to meet for fourteen months with a federal mediator. The case was permitted to move into the litigation process only after the federal mediator concluded that the parties would be unable to reach agreement through mediation alone.[19] Entry into the civil litigation process does not end negotiation, but merely initiates a new negotiation process within the structured environment of the court in which the judge can supervise and shape the parties' discussions through interim decisions about contested issues. During pretrial processes, when judges make decisions about which issues and evidence will be relevant to the case, such decisions tend to strengthen the position of one or the other of the parties and thereby place greater pressure upon the opposing party to undertake good faith negotiations in search of a settlement that will avoid the risk of complete defeat at trial.

The litigation process may not be entirely adversarial because the interests of various actors are at issue. Although the state government will fight against prison reform litigation, individual correctional administrators quietly accept specific aspects of such litigation. Because corrections systems are often a low priority in state governmental budgets and therefore may be seriously underfunded, judicial intervention applies pressure upon legislatures to provide needed resources for the officials who administer correctional institutions. This is not to say that prison administrators actually support prison litigation. They generally object to overly intrusive judicial orders that interfere with the daily operations of prisons. They also object to the overall diminution of their symbolic and actual authority over inmates and staff that results from an outsider (the judge) undercutting their control of decisions and policies within an institution.[20] For correctional administrators, the added resources that may result from judicial intervention may be a beneficial consequence of an objectionable process.

In some circumstances in which corrections officials agree that their institutions need the reforms sought through litigation, they may cooperate with the plaintiffs and the court in developing and implementing remedies. The ability of officials to cooperate freely may be limited by the officials' concerns about external constituencies such as legislators and voters, who may not understand that correctional institutions need to meet constitutional standards. The need to meet standards is not simply for the benefit of the prisoners, but also to insure the effective and safe operation of the institutions for the officials who work there. For example, if prisoners' morale is low because of complaints about poor living conditions, there is a risk of uprisings that will endanger the staff as well as the inmates. In addition, corrections officials have been affected by the professionalization movement that has altered the composition, training, and goals of police officers and other government service workers. The contemporary corrections officials who have professional training in criminological theory and other advanced subjects often hope to improve their institutions to meet the recommended standards established by the American Corrections Association. Thus the administrators' professional reform goals may overlap with those of the prisoner-plaintiffs. When the contending parties share common interests, the judge may be able to facilitate an agreement on implementing reforms. In one case, for example, jail administrators and interest group lawyers agreed that an old jail needed a fire escape. The judicial officer cooperated with the parties to facilitate communication about feasible solutions and to educate local elected officials about the need for remodeling the jail to meet constitutional standards.[21]

Even in adversarial cases that go to trial and result in judicial decisions against correctional institutions, there are opportunities for the parties to interact and participate in developing and implementing solutions. In litigation concerning conditions in an Ohio prison, for example, the judge did not impose his own remedy, but instead asked the state to propose alternative remedies for the prison overcrowding problem.[22] In the Alabama state prison litigation, the judge initially appointed a thirty-nine-member Human Rights Committee to oversee the implementation of prison reform. The chairperson of the committee and the committee's professional consultant met regularly with the judge, attorneys for the state, and attorneys for prisoners in order to implement the substantial reforms.[23] The committee was not only a vehicle for supervising and interacting with the contending parties during the implementation phase, "it was an instrument through which Judge [Frank] Johnson brought prominent and frequently outspoken citizens into the process, broadening public awareness about conditions in Alabama's prisons."[24]

Special Masters and Other Participants

Judges frequently appoint "special masters" or "monitors," often law school professors or others with expertise on criminal justice issues, to supervise the implementation of remedies. In the Georgia State Prison case, which resulted in a settlement decree rather than a trial and judicial decision, the special master supervised the implementation of reforms and served as the focal point for negotiated settlements between the parties:

> [The monitor was appointed] with the consent of the parties. . . . [He] was given broad powers beyond mere oversight of decree implementation and acted as fact-finder, mediator, manager, and planner. . . . [He] drafted a series of reports on the [state's] . . . compliance. Negotiated decrees were issued throughout this period. In the process the monitor interpreted these decrees and

refined their scope by setting the criteria for measuring compliance.[25]

Prison administrators have complained, however, that "even casual examination of the background of masters who have been used in the leading prison cases raises substantial doubts about whether they have managerial skills or significant correctional knowledge."[26]

In prison reform litigation, the interactions that result in negotiated settlements or in policy development after a judicial decision do not include merely the judge and the attorneys for the contending parties. A study of the Georgia case identified thirty-six key decision makers, including various prison wardens, state-level officials, federal government officials, outside interest groups, and the attorneys and judicial personnel.[27] Although litigation is often viewed as a conflict between two parties under the supervision of a judge, the litigation and negotiation processes for prison reform litigation may contain representation from a variety of differing interests. Because reform litigation and its concomitant negotiation processes often drag on for years, there are "generational" problems as personnel representing the various perspectives leave their positions and are replaced by newcomers to the case. In the Georgia case, for example, "[d]ifferent generations of litigation teams would often have little knowledge of what earlier participants had done."[28] The length of the litigation process, which took fourteen years in the Georgia example, can undercut the potential effectiveness of judicial policy-making by hampering continuity among relevant actors. The litigation process itself is not the source of all delay, however. Because institutional reform litigation may involve expensive renovations of old prisons, there are frequently time lags lasting several (or many) years as legislatures act to allocate money and the building projects are undertaken with continued monitoring by the federal courts.

Judges' Decisions

The gravest risk that judges will go "too far" arises in cases that move through trial to judicial decision. The basis for judicial decisions in reform litigation has been vague legal tests that ask such questions as whether the "totality of conditions" within prisons "shock the conscience."[29] Such vague standards do not provide clear guidance to either judges or correctional officials about what standards must be achieved within prisons. In effect, vague standards give judges greater authority to issue decisions and shape negotiations according to their own personal sense of appropriate constitutional standards for prison conditions:

> Typically a trial court opinion in a conditions case reads more like a consultant's report than a legal opinion. . . . The core of the opinion is a detailed description of conditions in the institution which emphasizes the gap between the magnitude of functions to be performed and the failings in the effort to perform them—lack of funds, lack of staff, incompetence, and the like. . . . Often the court characterizes conditions and services in graphic detail and concludes that they are "brutal," "savage," "barbaric," or "horrifying" and then orders the institution to take immediate steps to rectify the situation, leaving a management plan to be worked out later, often by the parties themselves or under the auspices of a special master.[30]

Although courts have struggled to develop standards, as the American Correctional Association, the American Medical Association, and other professional organizations have developed model standards for such matters as facilities and medical services in prisons, "courts have incorporated these emerging professional norms into their orders rather than inventing their own requirements."[31] Despite the perception that judicial intervention into corrections stems from the activism of politically liberal judges, in fact, both Republican and Democratic federal judges appointed by conservative and liberal presidents have been involved in prison reform cases.[32] Apparently conditions in correctional institutions have been sufficiently disturbing to strike judges from various political backgrounds as violations of the Constitution.

Most judges have sought to maintain a balanced judicial role in order to pressure deficient correctional systems to reform but permit participants in the case to develop feasible remedies. An early study of several prison reform cases found:

> [T]he judges perceived their role as limited to ordering changes that would raise conditions to constitutionally acceptable levels. Consequently, formulation of relief to be ordered involved coming to terms with two sets of realities: the need to develop remedies for extreme abuses . . . and the need for remedies that were realistic and achievable within the social and political context. . . . Each court attempted to evoke a willing response to the duties that were contained in its orders. . . . The courts wished to avoid judicial intervention in executive and legislative functions and to minimize whatever intervention was necessary. They stressed that intervention had been forced upon them by the inaction of responsible [state officials].[33]

Although some judges are willing to involve themselves in the day-to-day operations of prisons if it seems necessary, it would be difficult to claim that judges are eager to undertake those responsibilities.

The Consequences of Judicial Intervention

Improved Standards and Conditions

In the aftermath of two decades of judicial intervention into correctional institutions, even critics of policy-making by courts concede that such intervention is associated with improved living conditions in prisons and the elimination of the worst aspects of brutality sanctioned by prison officials.[34] Although some may argue that the new generation of professional corrections administrators undertook many reforms on their own initiative,[35] the extent of improvements in prison conditions and practices would not have been achieved without judicial intervention. The efforts of the American Correctional Association and other professional associations to develop accreditation standards for prisons were a response to litigation.[36] Judges, in turn, drew from these professionally developed standards in creating guidelines for subsequent decisions in prison cases. Court cases provided the basis for shining a light at the dark corners behind the walls of correctional institutions so that external evaluators (i.e., judges) and the public could become aware of the problems and abuses within prisons. Moreover, the assertions of judicial power pushed state and local governments to supply needed resources for correctional institutions and to adopt professional standards for the training of personnel and maintenance of constitutional conditions. As one study of prison reform concluded about judicial intervention:

> The prison's boundaries had become permeable to the outside. Local control had been lost to centralized authority and the universalistic rule of law. The new emphasis on bureaucratization prescribed professional standards of preparation for a new administrative elite.[37]

Violence and Disorder

Institutional change cannot be implemented easily, so changes in standards and conditions are not the only consequences of judicial intervention. Despite the positive consequences associated with judicial intervention, prison reform litigation also leads to new problems that raise lingering questions about whether judges undertake proper courses of action while intervening in the administration of correctional institutions.

Some studies indicate that judicial intervention into correctional institutions is associated with increases in violence. Judicial orders may raise inmate expectations about benefits that they are to receive while simultaneously undercutting the authority of the existing administrative structure in the eyes of both prisoners and staff.[38] In addition, problems arise because judicial decrees forbid correctional officers from continuing to employ violent, physical punishments as the means to control inmate behavior. This upheaval in the authority structure coincided with new assertiveness by prisoners and the development of gang activity within correctional institutions.

> Changes mandated by the court in *Ruiz* led to the feeling among both inmates and staff that the balance of power within prison had shifted in the inmates' favor. This shift, coupled with greater uncertainty among staff stemming from less experience and a new set of rules for applying disciplinary measures, led to an increased hesitancy on the part of staff to intervene in inmate-inmate confrontations. . . . [Violence escalated] as gangs attempted to establish dominance and inmates increasingly relied on self-protection in the face of what was perceived as the weakened position of the staff.[39]

Although there is evidence of increases in violence during and immediately after reform litigation, other studies indicate that such violence may be merely a short-term consequence of judicial intervention as a prison's new organizational structures and procedures are implemented.[40]

Financial Costs and Effects on State Budgets

Compliance with judicial orders can be expensive. Because judicial intervention may push state and local governments to spend more money on corrections, government officials may be faced with the choice of removing funding from other programs or raising taxes.[41] Although one scholar has argued that judicial intervention into corrections has had only modest overall effects on state governmental budgets,[42] it is clear that prison reform litigation has had a significant effect upon expenditures for corrections in the South. As Malcolm Feeley notes, "[t]his is no mean achievement for a section of the country where for years officials had rejected as a matter of principle the 'expensive luxury' of using state funds to house prisoners and where 'all deliberate speed' once meant a snail's pace."[43] Although judicial influence over states' taxing and spending policies, the traditional domain of elected officials, is highly controversial, such judicial intervention succeeded in pushing many states to catch up with the rest of the country in implementing standards for conditions in prisons.[44] Prior to the initiation of litigation in the 1960s and 1970s, some states spent as little as possible on prisons by permitting armed prisoners to serve as corrections officers. These prisoners controlled, exploited, and abused other prisoners with state-sanctioned brutality. Judges might not have felt compelled to enter into the uncomfortable and difficult situation of affecting state budgetary decisions if the public had more awareness and concern about the problems within prisons. According to one prison administrator, "[o]nce the public is informed, and comes to expect basic decency in the jails and prisons, the legislative support in funding will not be far behind."[45] In an era of increasing public fear and anger about crime, however, it seems unlikely that the public will actually push legislators to do anything other than punish offenders more severely.

Increased Litigation

Judicial intervention into prisons may also encourage prisoners to file more and more legal actions in the hope that judges will make additional improvements in conditions or otherwise provide new benefits for inmates. Since the 1960s, the federal courts' receptivity to prisoners' cases has been associated with dramatic increases in case filings. In 1960, prior to judicial intervention into prison reform litigation, there were only 2,177 cases filed by prisoners in federal district courts. By 1990, after courts had evaluated prison policies for more than two decades, there were 42,630 cases filed.[46] This litigation exacts a substantial cost from both the corrections and the judicial systems. Corrections officials and state attorneys general constantly instruct their agencies' attorneys to investigate complaints and file responses to prisoners' allegations. For those complaints that survive preliminary dismissal, government attorneys must meet in pretrial conferences, conduct discovery, and engage in the other activities associated with the long and expensive processes of civil litigation. Court clerks, law clerks, and judicial officers in the federal courts must spend time filing, processing, and reading the thousands of petitions filed by prisoners. Because the federal courts have experienced accelerating growth in civil cases during the same time period, the burden of prisoners' petitions may detract from adequate judicial consideration of all cases and, thereby encourage routinized decision making.

It would be inaccurate, however, to view the growth in prisoners' petitions solely as a consequence of judicial intervention into prisons. Because the increase in prisoners' filings during the 1980s has coincided with a huge increase in prison populations due to increased severity in sentencing, the burdens upon the federal courts are also a natural consequence of prison population growth rather than simply judicial encouragement of litigation. For example, although state prison populations increased by 144 percent between 1970 and 1984, prisoner filings during that period increased only 125 percent.[47] To many observers, the basic problem is not that courts encourage lawsuits, but that correctional institutions have failed to develop grievance procedures and alternative mechanisms for prisoners to seek redress of their complaints.[48] Congress enacted the Civil Rights of Institutionalized Persons Act, which empowered the U.S. attorney general and federal courts to certify that prisons have proper grievance procedures and thereby force prisoners to utilize those procedures before pursuing litigation.[49] Although this statute could reduce the litigation burdens upon government officials and courts, very few states have implemented certifiably proper procedures.

The Future of Judicial Intervention

Prison reform litigation has been exceptionally controversial because some judges have become deeply involved in administrative and budgetary decisions that are normally executive branch functions. Even critics of judicial intervention concede, however, that the flagrant abuses in many prisons required outside intervention. Judicial officers who heard evidence about inhuman treatment and conditions in correctional institutions, including conservative Republican judges and liberal Democratic judges, felt that they had no choice but to take some kind of action. They could not simply wait for legislative and executive branch officials to remedy the very problems that those same officials had created and maintained in the first place.[50] Because the American public possesses little knowledge or concern about conditions within prisons, there have been few incentives for elected officials to devote attention to problems within corrections systems. Judicial policy-making has provided the push for the professionalization of prison administration and the development of standards for conditions within prisons.

It is easy to identify cases that raise questions about whether individual judges went too far in supervising the day-to-day administrative decisions within prisons. As judges felt their way along in addressing prison reform, it was difficult to strike the proper balance between adequate judicial supervision to ensure timely compliance with needed improvements and appropriate judicial deference to the expertise of correctional administrators. In retrospect, it may have been better for judges to take a more incremental approach in forcing changes within prisons.[51] However, any changes in correctional institutions will cause some degree of upheaval, so there is no perfect formula for judges to follow when shaping correctional policies.

Judicial policy-making in prisons tends to evolve from negotiation between the parties. Although early cases forced judges to issue strong decisions in the face of significant resistance from correctional officials, most cases do not fit a stereotypical image of adversarial courtroom battles leading to victory for one side. The expense and difficulty of reforming prisons and the overriding need to maintain institutional security encourages judges to invite participation by correctional officials in the process of developing and implementing new policies. The process is not one of equal or free negotiation between the parties. Judges will structure the negotiations to push the correctional administrators toward attainment of certain prison conditions. These conditions are established by the courts through reliance upon outside experts and are based upon the standards developed by professional associations. As in other policy issues affected by judicial action, judges are not dictators imposing their wills upon other branches of government. Judges are certainly powerful actors in shaping the goals to be attained and pushing the other governmental branches toward those goals. However, the processes and consequences of judicial intervention into prison reform inevitably involve complex interactions between various interested parties over long periods of time. Prison reform through judicial intervention is time-consuming, inefficient, and can lead to unintended consequences, such as short-term increases in violence and impacts upon allocation of governmental funds. Despite these flaws, courts play a critical role in initiating needed reforms for problems that, by nature, are unlikely to capture sufficient attention and concern from the public and elected officials in order to generate the necessary political action for reform by other branches of government.

Prison litigation has resulted in the development of general standards for the treatment of prisoners. With the departure of old-style authoritarian prison wardens during the 1970s and the increased influence of educated, professional correctional administrators, there is less need for judicial intervention into prisons. In addition, decisions by the U.S. Supreme Court have placed limits upon the extent to which federal judges can intervene into the affairs of correctional institutions.[52] Through the appointment of more conservative judicial officers by Republican presidents, the political system responded to fears of excessive judicial activism by imposing constraints upon potential actions by judges to shape criminal justice policies. Despite these developments that have reduced the controversy surrounding judicial involvement in prison reform, there will continue to be prison reform cases directed at one issue in particular: prison and jail over-crowding. Because of the dramatically escalating prison populations during the 1980s (329,821 in 1980 to 710,054 in 1989)[53] and continuing into the 1990s, courts will be called upon to evaluate overcrowding problems within prisons. Although courts will continue to impose ceilings upon jail and prison capacity, they are not likely to dictate the details of societal policy responses to growing prison populations. As in earlier prison litigation in which negotiation played such an impor-tant behind-the-scenes role, the courts will be one actor in the continu-ing series of complex interactions between sheriffs, wardens, governors, legislatures, interest groups, taxpayers, and other inter-ested parties. By defining the boundaries of acceptable policies (e.g., how many prisoners can be inside one jail or prison), courts push other actors in the political system to develop the specific policies that will accomplish American society's goals of punishing offenders more severely while limiting government expenditures on corrections. The consequences of continued judicial pressure upon policymakers are likely to be not only the construction of additional prisons, but further development of less expensive alternatives such as electronically monitored home detention, "boot camps" for young offenders, and increased use of fines and restitution. Now that standards and limita-tions have been developed for judicial policy-making in correctional administration, courts are likely to be catalysts for innovation by other policymakers rather than acting themselves as inventors and directors of policy initiatives.

CHAPTER 7
ABORTION: THE JUDICIARY'S INTERACTIONS WITH OTHER POLITICAL ACTORS

JUDICIAL DECISIONS AFFECTING abortion policy thrust the judiciary into a nearly unprecedented storm of political controversy. According to Archibald Cox, "[no court decision] except the *Dred Scott* case[1] [concerning slavery] has aroused as intense popular emotion. Few have raised more profound questions concerning the role of the Supreme Court of the United States in American government."[2] Abortion represents a controversial issue about which American society is deeply and seemingly irreconcilably divided. It is difficult to identify a compromise position on the abortion issue that might generate agreement between the highly-mobilized competing interests groups that, respectively, vocally support and adamantly oppose a woman's right to choose to terminate a pregnancy.

The U.S. Supreme Court unleashed years of intense political maneuvering and conflict when it utilized its authority over constitutional interpretation to define abortion as a protected right under the Constitution. In the landmark case of *Roe v. Wade*,[3] the Court supported a woman's challenge against a Texas statute that made it a criminal offense to obtain or attempt an abortion, unless the mother's life was endangered by the pregnancy. Justice Harry Blackmun's opinion for the Court identified a right of choice for abortion during the first six months of pregnancy as a component of the constitutional right to privacy. During the second trimester of pregnancy (months four through six), states were permitted to regulate how abortions would be performed in order to protect the health of women, but states could not bar abortions prior to the seventh month of pregnancy when the fetus was regarded as "viable," capable of living outside of the mother's womb. Because of its breadth, the Supreme Court's opinion effectively cast aside statutes regulating or banning abortions in dozens of states. Although the *Roe* decision was controversial, a solid seven-member majority on the Court supported abortion as a protected right under the Constitution.

The Supreme Court did not initiate the national debate on abortion. As with other policy issues, abortion was the subject of growing policy battles in various political arenas throughout the country before it reached the highest court through litigation. For example, a few state legislatures including Hawaii,[4] had begun to liberalize their abortion laws in response to interest group pressures and changing societal attitudes about women's rights. Although the Supreme Court did not create the abortion controversy, it was the first national policy-making institution to make a broad, authoritative declaration on the subject. The Court placed abortion high on the national policy agenda and forced other national political institutions to become involved with this policy issue.

In the years following the *Roe* decision, the judicial branch found itself faced with the abortion issue in various forms again and again. The abortion issue, as much as any other policy issue, illustrates the limited ability of the courts to finalize policy judgments. Because the judicial branch is a component of the larger political system, judicial influence over policy-making is affected by the judiciary's interactions with other interested political actors and governmental institutions.

Mobilization of Interest Groups

The Supreme Court's decision in *Roe v. Wade* defined national abortion policy in a manner that clashed with the views of a large minority of the American population. Many religious denominations, most notably the Catholic Church, believe that abortion is impermissible because it entails ending a human life. Because this minority believed strongly that the Supreme Court's policy decision was wrong, politically active anti-abortion interest groups "took the initiative after 1973 in a forceful counteroffensive against abortion."[5] These interest groups sponsored public relations campaigns, protest marches, and lobbying efforts aimed at persuading elected officials and the general public to oppose the pro-choice policy established by the Supreme Court's decision.

Interest groups supporting women's right of choice had worked during the 1960s to reform the strict abortion statutes in many states. After the Supreme Court's decision favoring their preferred public policy position, many of these groups erroneously believed that they had won the policy debate:

> [T]he pro-choice groups, while active in the late 1960s in opposing state abortion laws, were late in beginning their advocacy after *Roe v. Wade* in 1973. Many in this movement felt that *Wade* had finally settled the issue of abortion. The pro-choice groups were not prepared for the intense counteroffensive launched by the pro-life groups. Thus much of what the pro-choice advocates did between 1973 and 1978 was in response to the pro-life movement.[6]

Eventually, the pro-choice organizations became very politically active as a means to protect and preserve the policy victory achieved in *Roe v. Wade*.

Interest Group Pressure and Judges' Decisions

The mobilization of interest group activities led to relatively intense public pressures upon the justices to alter their decision favoring choice in abortions:

> In the years immediately following *Roe*, hundreds of thousands of letters arrived at the Court, some congratulating but most condemning the justices. Blackmun alone received more than forty-five thousand letters, and he was seriously troubled by the attacks on him as the "Butcher of Dachau, murderer, Pontius Pilate, Adolf Hitler." Threats were made on his life. As a result, security at the Court was increased, and more protection given to justices when they traveled to and from the Court.[7]

Despite the pressure, Blackmun remained a staunch defender of his opinion in *Roe*.

Other justices differed in their views about whether it was proper for interest groups to attempt to exert pressure directly upon the judicial branch. When asked about whether he objected to demonstrators marching around the Supreme Court, Justice Lewis Powell believed that it was good for people to be interested and involved in issues of public controversy: "Frequently, there are demonstrations around the [C]ourt. In our democratic system, that is a plus."[8] According to Powell, "[I]f you are a federal judge appointed for life, you are not likely to be influenced by people marching around the [C]ourt."[9]

By contrast, Justice Antonin Scalia was very disturbed at the sight of demonstrators around the courthouse. Because he felt that the public should not treat courts as "political" institutions, he argued that the judiciary should not make policy decisions affecting abortion. Scalia bemoaned the fact that by continuing their involvement in the abortion issue, the justices must look forward to "another Term with carts full of mail from the public, and streets full of demonstrators" urging the justices to change their decisions.[10] Despite his concerns about the "great damage to the Court['s image]" from political activities directed at the judicial branch, Scalia did not believe that such activities directly affect justices' decisions.[11]

As indicated in the discussion of school desegregation cases in chapter 4, public reactions or anticipated reactions to judicial decisions can affect judges' decision making. Judges may formulate policy pronouncements in a manner that avoids risking massive resistance by moderating the speed or form of implementation. In the case of abortion, however, the public pressure had little direct effect on judicial decisions because only a minority of the public strongly opposes abortion. Public opinion research indicates that most Americans' views on abortion are situated between those of the two polar extremes of the organized interests that vociferously defend and stridently oppose abortion.[12] Thus, judicial decision makers do not face the same potential for massive resistance that existed in school desegregation. Moreover, unlike school desegregation, a policy in which implementation required the cooperation of broad segments of the American public, abortion can be easily implemented because only willing, supportive individuals are involved in procuring and providing abortions. The opponents of abortion made attempts to disrupt implementation through means ranging from picketing and sit-ins to the firebombing of abortion clinics.[13] Any disobedience to the law, however, generally resulted in swift, consistent law enforcement actions against the protestors and did not halt the availability of abortion.

Legislative Reactions to Judicial Policy-Making

Interest group activities outside of the judicial process have little direct effect upon judicial decisions, but such activities can influence judicial policy-making by generating legislative reactions to court decisions. The anti-abortion interests succeeded in persuading Congress and state legislatures to challenge the judicial policy announced in *Roe v. Wade*. Because any single judicial decision cannot provide complete and comprehensive answers to all of the questions and circumstances that may arise concerning a particular policy issue, other political actors can create new challenges to the policy that lead the courts to reconsider and refine initial policy decisions: "Like most Supreme Court policy-making, *Roe* left numerous questions unanswered and afforded ample opportunities for thwarting compliance with its mandate."[14] As Louis Fisher observed, "*Roe v. Wade* has not been accepted as the 'last word' on the rights of abortion. Legislative efforts by state and local bodies put constant pressure on the Court to clarify and modify the boundaries of its 1973 ruling."[15] Through new legislation, opponents of *Roe* could raise specific issues concerning abortion that would become the focal points for additional court cases. The issues raised in these new cases might divide the Supreme Court or lead specific justices to reconsider their initial support for a right to choose abortion.

Members of Congress reacted to the decision in *Roe v. Wade* by threatening a variety of legislative proposals aimed at changing the abortion policy announced by the Supreme Court. The legislative efforts to initiate a constitutional amendment to ban abortion and to limit judicial jurisdiction over abortion issues never gained sufficient support within the legislature for enactment.[16] Congress did succeed, however, in passing legislation that barred federal government funding for abortions sought by poor women. Such legislation aimed at modifying a controversial judicial policy inevitably generates new cases in the court system that test the strength and breadth of the judges' original decision. As many scholars have noted, courts do not necessarily finalize the policies that they develop. Judges must constantly reassess those policies as reactions by other political actors and institutions generate new cases within the courts that present new challenges to judicial policies.[17] After the enactment of Congressional restrictions on abortion funding, a deeply divided Supreme Court limited the effective availability of abortions for poor women by approving the legislative ban on federally funded abortions.[18] The Court also declared that the U.S. Constitution permitted state legislatures to impose similar limitations upon the use of state funds for poor women's abortions.[19]

State and local legislative bodies attempted to make even more significant and direct challenges to the Supreme Court's decision in *Roe*. From 1973 to 1989, the Supreme Court consistently struck down a series of city and state laws that attempted to limit the availability of abortion. The City of Akron, Ohio, for example, passed a municipal ordinance that purported to comply with *Roe's* provision for reasonable regulations designed to protect the health of the mother during the second trimester of pregnancy. The ordinance sought to impose several restrictions upon abortions within the city:

> (1) all abortions performed after the first trimester had to be performed in a hospital, (2) abortions were prohibited for unmarried minors under age 15 without parental consent or court order, (3) the physician had to inform the woman of various facts concerning the operation, (4) abortions were delayed for at least twenty-four hours after the woman's consent, and (5) the physician had to insure that fetal remains were disposed of in a "humane and sanitary manner."[20]

On the surface, these restrictions had an appearance of reasonableness, but the underlying details within the city's restrictions included direct challenges to the Supreme Court's decision in *Roe*. Most notably, the ordinance required doctors to inform women that "the unborn child is a human life from the moment of conception."[21] This provision clashed directly with the Court's opinion in *Roe*. The Supreme Court had expressly stated in *Roe* that the beginning of human life could not be precisely defined: "When those trained in the respective disciplines of medicine, philosophy, and theology are unable to arrive at a consensus, the judiciary, at this point in the development of man's knowledge, is not in a position to speculate as to the [beginning point of life]."[22] The Court had little patience with thinly-disguised attacks upon its policy decision and it struck down the entire Akron ordinance as well as other state and local laws that attempted to regulate abortion and thereby hinder women's choices.[23]

For fifteen years, the anti-abortion efforts met with relatively little success in challenging the judicial policy endorsing abortion. By keeping abortion on the national policy agenda, however, the interest groups could keep pressuring other political actors to oppose the judicial policy. Eventually, because of the judiciary's connections with the political system, developments affecting other branches of government led to changes in the judicial policy concerning abortion.

Presidential Appointment Power and the Composition of the Judiciary

Anti-abortion interests became visible, powerful elements within the Republican Party. They helped to place an anti-abortion statement in the party platform and they worked vigorously on behalf of Republican candidates who opposed abortion. In 1980, their efforts helped to elect Ronald Reagan, an abortion opponent, to the presidency. Reagan was not elected because of his position on abortion. In fact, most of the public disagreed with Reagan's stated desire to ban abortions. People voted for Reagan for a variety of reasons, including President Jimmy Carter's negative image in the eyes of the public, the hostage crisis in Iran, dissatisfaction with taxes, and other policy issues. Although they voted for Reagan for a variety of other reasons, by virtue of his election to the presidency, the American voters effectively gave anti-abortion interests access to the policy-shaping powers of the most important elective office in the country.

Although President Reagan supported constitutional amendment proposals and legislation to limit the availability of abortion, such mechanisms did not have much impact on abortion policy. The Reagan administration presented anti-abortion arguments to the Supreme Court whenever cases arose concerning state statutes that challenged the decision in *Roe*.[24] These arguments did not persuade the Court to make major changes in *Roe*. Reagan ultimately had significant influence over the reshaping of abortion policy through the specific presidential power that can have the greatest impact upon judicial policy formulation—the power to appoint federal judges.

The Reagan administration made the transformation of the judiciary one of its highest priorities. Reagan's assistants made a concerted effort to appoint judges who shared the administration's views on a variety of policy issues, including opposition to abortion. Moreover, Reagan appointed young judges to the federal bench, including some as young as thirty-two years of age, in order to insure that they would continue to shape the development of conservative judicial policies long after Reagan left office.[25]

Because law is not composed of fixed, neutral principles of justice, judges' interpretations of constitutions, statutes, and previous court decisions define the meaning of law—and of public policy. Social science studies on judicial decision making show very clearly that judges shape and change the development of law and judicial policies according to their personal values, attitudes, and policy preferences.[26] Thus the Reagan appointees, with their conservative values, were able to begin the process of reshaping judicial policy decisions on abortion in a manner that restricted the availability of the right of choice established in *Roe v. Wade*. A study of abortion case decisions in the federal district courts documented that "the Reagan appointees were much more resistant to abortion rights than were the appointees of his predecessors, including the appointees of fellow Republican Richard Nixon."[27]

By serving two complete terms in office, Reagan had the opportunity to appoint an unprecedented number of judges to the federal bench. At the end of his term, Reagan had appointed 377 of the 752 federal judges.[28] This legacy of appointing conservative, anti-abortion judges to the federal courts was subsequently continued by George Bush's administration. President Bush chose to employ similar ideological screening methods when selecting judicial nominees.[29] As a result, the lower levels of the federal courts became substantially comprised of judges who were selected, in part, because they were expected to oppose the abortion policy established in *Roe v. Wade*. This "packing" of the federal courts created new trends in judicial decisions affecting the right of choice in abortion as well as other policies affecting individuals' rights.[30] Although the Supreme Court can ultimately control many fundamental decisions about law and policy, the lower courts have significant influence over the policy consequences of most individual cases because the Supreme Court is able to hear only a relatively small number of cases each year. For example, during 1989–90 term, the Supreme Court accepted only 148 cases for complete hearing and decision.[31] Thus, the federal district courts and circuit courts of appeals affect the outcomes in most of the more than 300,000 cases filed in the federal courts each year.

The presidential appointment power constitutes a powerful tool for the political party that controls the White House to use in counteracting judicial policy decisions with which it disagrees. The Reagan administration exploited this tool with calculated thoroughness as a means to change judicial policies affecting such issues as affirmative action, school desegregation, and employment discrimination as well as abortion.

Reagan's Appointments to the Supreme Court

Although lower court judges have influence over the majority of outcomes produced by the courts, the justices of the Supreme Court are, literally and figuratively, the leaders of judicial policy-making. Their decisions shape and constrain the decisions made by lower court judges. Moreover, their decisions have the greatest symbolic and practical impacts upon the American public because of the inordinate level of media attention directed at the highest court. Reagan's greatest effectiveness in altering the judicial policy on abortion announced in *Roe v. Wade* came through his opportunities to replace several justices on the Supreme Court.

Justice Potter Stewart, a moderate Republican who had been appointed by President Dwight Eisenhower in the 1950s, retired in

1981. Reagan fulfilled a campaign promise designed to improve his standing with female voters by appointing the first woman justice of the Supreme Court, Sandra Day O'Connor. Although Justice O'Connor had impeccable conservative credentials as a Republican state senator and appellate judge in Arizona, she faced her greatest opposition during her confirmation hearings from anti-abortion interest groups that feared she would not seek to undo *Roe v. Wade*: "The Moral Majority and the National Right to Life Committee attacked her because as a state legislator she had supported a 'family planning' bill that would have repealed Arizona's statutes prohibiting abortions."[32] O'Connor subsequently pleased the anti-abortion groups and raised their expectations about her opposition to abortion when she wrote a dissenting opinion in 1983 that was sharply critical of the reasoning employed in the majority opinion in *Roe*.[33]

Because the interest groups that mobilized in the wake of *Roe* worked so hard to keep abortion as the central controversy on the national policy agenda, Senate confirmation hearings for Supreme Court nominees became a focal point for political battles concerning abortion. The opposition to O'Connor's nomination based upon a single policy issue generated a national debate about whether or not nominees should be approved or rejected based upon one controversial issue when justices' responsibilities actually involve making decisions about a broad range of issues.[34] Despite broad debate about whether abortion should be a litmus test for candidates, interest groups succeeded in pushing abortion as *the* issue that Supreme Court nominees must address in their confirmation hearings. Abortion remained a key issue in subsequent confirmation hearings, especially when the new appointee was likely to change markedly the existing ideological balance on the Court. In 1990, for example, abortion was a central focus of the hearings concerning President Bush's nomination of David Souter to replace retiring Justice William Brennan.[35] In 1991, the same issue was a key focal point for the Senate Judiciary Committee's questioning of Clarence Thomas, the justice who replaced Justice Thurgood Marshall.

In 1986, Reagan elevated the most conservative justice on the Supreme Court, William Rehnquist, to replace Warren Burger as Chief Justice. Rehnquist's position on abortion was clear. He was one of the two original dissenters in *Roe v. Wade* and he dissented consistently against subsequent Court decisions supporting the right of choice for abortion. As chief justice, however, Rehnquist gained the power to lead the discussion of cases and, when he was in the majority, to decide which justice would write the Court's opinion. Although the chief justice has always been characterized as merely "first among equals" rather than the "boss" of the other justices, chief justices in the past had been able to lead the Court in some decisions through effective use of the authority to guide discussions and make opinion assignments. Thus Rehnquist gained powers that could be employed to advance his views about abortion policy.

Antonin Scalia, an outspoken former law professor, was appointed to fill the vacancy left by the retirement of Chief Justice Burger. Scalia declined to answer specific questions about his views when he appeared before the Senate Judiciary Committee during his confirmation hearings. Because he was a conservative replacing another conservative on the Court and therefore would not change the Court's ideological balance of power for judicial policy-making, the senators did not press Scalia for his views. All observers accurately predicted that Scalia would oppose the established judicial policy on abortion.

When President Reagan nominated Robert Bork to replace retiring Justice Powell in 1987, abortion emerged again as a primary focus for the confirmation hearings. Bork's nomination was opposed by an array of interest groups, including pro-choice groups, because his well-known judicial philosophy made him a critic of many civil rights decisions issued by the Supreme Court. More than any other nominee, Bork was critical of the Court's development of a constitutional right to privacy that served as the basis for the judicial policy decision in *Roe v. Wade*.[36] The interest group campaign against Bork was successful and his nomination was defeated in the Senate by a vote of fifty-eight to forty-two.

After President Reagan's disastrous nomination of Douglas Ginsburg, who withdrew his nomination after it was revealed that he had smoked marijuana while serving as a professor at Harvard Law School, Anthony Kennedy was nominated to replace Justice Powell. Kennedy declined to answer specific questions about abortion during his confirmation hearings. He was easily confirmed by the Senate because, unlike Bork, he was not perceived as a strident ideologue. Conservatives expected Kennedy to provide the vote needed to change established liberal judicial policies and liberals hoped that he would prove to be a moderate.

Webster v. Reproductive Health Services

In 1989, the Reagan strategy succeeded in changing the Supreme Court's decisions affecting abortion policy. Of the seven justices who supported the majority opinion in *Roe v. Wade* in 1973, three were replaced by Reagan's appointees during the 1980s. When the three Reagan appointees (O'Connor, Scalia, and Kennedy) joined together with the two dissenters from the *Roe* decision (Rehnquist and White), they had enough votes to reshape the policy established by Justice Blackmun's opinion in 1973. The vehicle for changing judicial policy concerning abortion arrived at the Supreme Court in the form of a Missouri statute that imposed several restrictions upon women's choices: prohibiting public employees and public hospitals from performing abortions except to save a mother's life; prohibiting public support for abortion counseling; and requiring viability tests after twenty weeks of pregnancy to determine if the fetus could live on its own.[37] In addition, the statute contained a preamble that declared "[t]he life of each human being begins at conception" and that Missouri laws shall be interpreted to give unborn children the same legal and constitutional rights as other persons.[38]

Prior to the appointment of Justice Kennedy, as the case concerning Akron's ordinance demonstrated, statutory attempts to define the beginning of human life would have been struck down by the Supreme Court. With the changed composition of the Court, however, the three Reagan appointees joined the two holdover dissenters from *Roe* to issue a divisive five to four decision upholding the Missouri statute. Although Justice Scalia argued strenuously in a concurring opinion that *Roe v. Wade* should be reversed, the other four members of the majority declined to reverse *Roe*. It is apparent from the justices' opinions that Justice O'Connor was not prepared to overturn *Roe*. As a result, the other justices in the majority were content to pretend that they had left *Roe* intact while they actually opened the way for states to regulate abortions. Blackmun and the others who supported *Roe* were left complaining in dissenting opinions that the Court majority had done away with a long-standing precedent without having the honesty or courage to admit what it was actually doing.

In subsequent cases, the Supreme Court reaffirmed its new willingness to approve abortion regulations. The ability of young women to obtain abortions freely was limited when the Court approved laws in several states requiring notification of parents or approval by state judges for women under age eighteen who wish to obtain abortions.[39] In another case, the Court narrowly approved the Bush administration's preferred interpretation of a federal law and thereby prevented federally funded family planning clinics from even mentioning abortion as an option to poor women seeking medical assistance.[40]

The Consequences of the New Judicial Policy

The *Webster* decision was a great victory for the anti-abortion interests that had worked so long and so hard to undo the judicial policy enunciated in *Roe v. Wade*. Although the Supreme Court had declined to formally reverse *Roe*, it had clearly invited states to begin regulating abortions in a manner that the previous majority on the Supreme Court would never have permitted prior to Justice Kennedy's appointment. The policy announced by the Court in 1973 had been changed because developments in the political system had permitted abortion opponents to help their favored candidate to gain the presidency. President Reagan then used the presidential appointment power to change the composition of the judiciary and thereby eventually to change the policy pronouncements issued by the judiciary.

After the *Webster* decision, the mobilized abortion interest groups, both pro-choice and anti-abortion, redoubled their efforts to influence the composition of the Supreme Court. When Justice Brennan, a member of the *Roe* majority, retired in 1990, his replacement, Justice Souter, was confronted with many questions concerning his views on abortion. Souter consistently declined to answer any questions concerning the issue of abortion, although he did answer questions concerning other controversial policy issues. Pro-choice groups ultimately were the only interest groups to appear before the Senate Judiciary Committee in order to urge that Souter's nomination be rejected because the nominee had not demonstrated that he supported women's right of choice. When Justice Thurgood Marshall retired in 1991, his replacement, Clarence Thomas, went to extreme lengths to avoid answering any questions about his views on abortion.

In 1992, although Justice Thomas joined the justices seeking to reverse *Roe*, Justice Souter, Justice O'Connor, and, surprisingly, Justice Kennedy coauthored a five-member, majority opinion (including Justices Blackmun and Stevens) which effectively reiterated the *Webster* decision by endorsing abortion regulations but declining to overturn *Roe*. Thus the Court continued to prohibit states from banning abortions.[41]

Although *Roe v. Wade* continued to exist as a symbolic declaration that abortion was a component of the constitutional right to privacy, anti-abortion advocates were mistaken to believe that the case remained as the primary barrier to their stated goal of outlawing abortions. The Supreme Court's decision in *Webster* effectively achieved the primary focus of the interest groups' goals: states were invited by the Court to begin regulating abortion. *Roe v. Wade* still precluded states from formally banning abortions, but the receptivity of the new majority on the Court to regulations appeared to give cities and states significant authority to limit the availability of abortion.

Despite the anti-abortion interests' success in reconstituting the Supreme Court and inviting state regulation after the *Webster* decision, abortion remained widely available throughout the United States. The lack of practical success for anti-abortion interests stemmed from the Supreme Court's role in shaping the nation's abortion policy. Because of the way in which legal issues concerning abortion are presented to the Supreme Court, the Court will never decide the fundamental issue of whether or not abortion will be allowed in the United States. As a matter of precision, what the Court actually decides is whether or not the Constitution permits *states* to regulate or ban abortion. Thus, contrary to the frequently stated expectations of abortion opponents, even if the composition of the Supreme Court changes completely to become composed entirely of abortion opponents who unanimously overturn *Roe v. Wade*, abortion will remain widely available in the United States.

Although the Supreme Court declared a national policy favoring women's right of choice in 1973 and protected abortion choices during the first six months of pregnancy until 1989, the Supreme Court does not control the existence of abortion. A withdrawal of influence by the Supreme Court, as evidenced in the *Webster* case, does not completely alter the existing abortion policy; it simply passes responsibility for abortion policy-making over to state legislatures. Thus, the continued existence of abortion is not attributable to judicial policy-making by the Supreme Court, but instead stems from changed societal attitudes about abortion that lead elected officials in many states to support the continued availability of abortion. In essence, even with their victories in the judicial arena, anti-abortion interests simply lack the widespread political support necessary to motivate state legislatures throughout the country to regulate or ban abortion.

Several state legislatures acted in the aftermath of the *Webster* decision to place severe restrictions upon the availability of abortion. Laws that restrict abortions without banning them can withstand judicial scrutiny but these laws still will not prevent abortions. Because pro-choice political interests and pro-choice public opinion are so strong in many states,[42] these states will not restrict abortions. As a result, restrictions on abortion in some states will simply force women to travel to another state in order to obtain abortions. Thus the actual policy consequence of a reversal of *Roe v. Wade* will only affect poor women and young women who live in restrictive states and who cannot afford to spend the time and money to travel to another state to obtain an abortion.[43] After such a protracted battle over judicial policy making on abortion, the ultimate outcomes from changes in abortion policy will have a surprisingly modest impact upon the availability of abortion.

The Influence of Other Political Actors at the State Level

As the Supreme Court limits its influence over abortion policy, other political actors become more important in determining policy concerning the availability of abortions. Obviously, state and local legislative bodies bear the primary responsibility for defining public policy concerning abortion when the federal courts step aside. These legislative bodies do not, however, possess complete control over the issue because other actors within state political systems can also influence policy outcomes. North Dakota's legislature, for example, voted in 1991 to ban abortions except in cases of rape, incest, or if the mother's life was in danger. The legislation was never implemented, however, because the governor of North Dakota, like the governor of Idaho in a similar situation, vetoed the legislation.[44] The withdrawal of federal judicial policy-making creates opportunities for governors and other actors to assert their values and policy preferences in an effort to shape or stop abortion-related legislation. For example, voters in Washington state passed a state-wide referendum to protect abortion rights within the state.[45]

The removal of federal courts' control over abortion policy does not mean that judicial policy-making on abortion will end. As chapter 5 discussed in regard to education financing, state courts can become policymakers by employing their authority over the interpretation of state constitutions and state statutes. In several important cases affecting abortion, even when the federal courts would have permitted state legislatures to withdraw public funding for poor women's abortions, state courts declared that poor women are protected against such actions by the provisions of state constitutions. In effect, several state courts have interpreted their state constitutions as providing broader abortion rights than those established in the U.S. Constitution. For example, in California,[46] Michigan,[47] and Florida,[48] state appellate courts relied upon their interpretations of state constitutions to thwart legislative efforts to implement restrictive abortion regulations that would have been approved by the U.S. Supreme Court.

Conclusion

Judicial policies are not immune from change. The issue of abortion illustrates how the judiciary's connections to the political system can lead to changes in judicially-established policies. Because abortion was such a controversial issue, the decision in *Roe v. Wade* mobilized various actors and institutions within the political system to work toward changing the national abortion policy established by the Supreme Court. The eventual success achieved by anti-abortion interests was, in many respects, illusory. After the composition of the Supreme Court changed and new decisions emerged, abortion continued to be widely available because state legislatures did not act to limit the availability of abortion.

The judicial decision in *Roe v. Wade* was a useful symbol for the competing interests that supported and opposed the right of choice. Support or opposition to *Roe v. Wade* provided an important issue that political candidates utilized to distinguish themselves from each other. The judicial policy embodied in the Supreme Court's decision gave opposing political interests a visible, motivational symbol. Because of its prominence and the highly-publicized nature of its decisions, the Supreme Court casts a giant shadow over the policy disputes that it enters. The Court helps to motivate and inspire interested groups, but because the Court does not necessarily control policy outcomes, success in the judicial arena does not insure satisfactory policy outcomes for the victorious interests. As demonstrated by the practical policy consequences of changes in the Supreme Court's opinions on abortion, other actors in the political system can enter the policy battlefield to exert significant influence over the definition of social policy.

It can take years to change judicial policies because the composition of the federal judiciary does not change quickly. However, the Reagan administration was successful in transforming the federal courts on the abortion issue within eight short years. The Reagan era example provides incentives for other political interests to pursue their policy preferences through exploitation of the important connections between the courts and the political system, especially through the use of the president's influence over the appointment of new judicial policymakers.

CHAPTER 8
TORT LAW: THE CUMULATIVE POLICY CONSEQUENCES OF LITIGATION

PREVIOUS CHAPTERS HAVE EXAMINED the impact of courts upon the development of public policy by focusing upon decisions made by judges who are confronted with policy issues in legal cases. In such circumstances, one of the parties initiates a legal action in order to seek a judge's approval of a policy position. Frequently, an individual files a claim against a governmental entity (e.g., school system, prison, state government, city government), alleging that actions by that governmental unit violate the dictates of the U.S. Constitution, a state constitution, or some other legal authority (i.e., case law or statutory law). When confronted with cases that directly raise policy issues, judges have the opportunity to consider their own interpretations of the Constitution's commands concerning such issues and the probable consequences for society that will result from particular decisions. Most discussions of judicial policy-making focus upon this process by which interested parties pursue policy objectives through litigation and thereby create opportunities for judges to make conscious decisions about public policy outcomes that are, in the judges' view, mandated by law. However, courts influence public policy developments in ways other than through this standard formulation of planned litigation designed to elicit decisions based upon judicial enforcement of con-

125

stitutional rights. The litigation process and judicial outcomes in cases concerning seemingly narrow disputes between private contending parties can have powerful cumulative impacts upon the distribution of costs and benefits throughout American society. In other words, litigation that was initiated merely to gain a financial recovery for a single individual can inadvertently affect the decisions, policies, and legal obligations of businesses, governments, and individuals throughout society.

Tort Law Litigation

Judicial decisions in a variety of areas of law can have effects beyond merely the two parties involved in a specific case. For example, court cases concerning the ownership and use of real estate can create new rules that affect the decisions of owners and potential purchasers of property. Judges' decisions that enforce or decline to enforce contracts send messages to others in society about the kinds of contractual relationships that can be protected through the judicial process. Although judicial decisions in many areas of law shape the policies that govern relationships, transactions, and the distribution of benefits among people within the United States, tort law cases have had a particularly significant impact upon American society. Tort litigation absorbs significant financial resources from American society. In 1985, it was estimated that total expenditures for tort litigation were between $29 billion and $36 billion, including attorneys' fees, court costs, and compensation paid to claimants.[1] Although these costs alone are significant, the cumulative effects of litigation extend beyond these estimatable costs to affect society through the immeasurable costs of increased insurance premiums nationwide and decreased availability of certain beneficial products and services. One insurance company claimed that the consequential costs of tort litigation amount to $80 billion annually.[2]

A "tort" is a civil wrong for which the law provides a remedy. People initiate tort lawsuits to recover "damages" for personal injuries, property losses, and various harms for which individuals, businesses, or other entities can be held legally responsible. There are many examples of tort actions. An individual who suffers physical injuries and incurs medical expenses from an automobile accident may file a tort lawsuit called a personal injury action. A person whose reputation or business prospects have been substantially harmed by the publication of false information may file a tort action for defamation (i.e., slander or libel). If someone is injured by a defective lawnmower or by improperly manufactured medicine, lawsuits may be filed against the companies that produced and sold the harmful products. In addition, any damage to a person's home, automobile, or other property may provide the basis for a property damage tort action against the responsible party. If someone prevails in a tort suit, they may be awarded "compensatory damages" for the economic harms that they actually suffered as well as "punitive damages," extra and frequently significant amounts of money intended to punish the wrongdoer and deter others from causing such harms.

The American system creates incentives for tort litigation that do not exist in other countries. American attorneys have a strong self-interest in filing tort lawsuits and seeking significant damage awards. Because attorneys receive a "contingency fee," normally 30 percent of any award or settlement, even poor plaintiffs can find enthusiastic representation for large tort cases. In other countries in which litigants must pay attorneys' fees directly or losing parties must pay the winning side's legal expenses, people may be more reluctant to initiate uncertain claims.[3] In addition, because Americans lack the universal health insurance and generous disability programs that protect people in European countries, people injured in the United States feel obligated to file lawsuits in order to recover for burdensome payments for medical, rehabilitation, and other expenses that can drain the family resources of Americans.[4]

Tort law cases are significant for public policy because they can change the rules for the behavior of individuals and businesses and also redistribute wealth throughout society. For example, in October 1991 a jury in Chicago awarded a man $127 million because he lost his left eye when a doctor injected the eye with a synthetic steroid drug.[5] The award included $3.1 million in actual compensatory damages for the loss of the eye and $124.5 million in punitive damages to punish the manufacturer of the steroid. Although the award subsequently may be reduced or overturned on appeal, if it stands, it may have significant cumulative effects upon other people in American society. The drug company may have to sell its factory and thereby jeopardize its employees' jobs in order to pay the award. The company may seek to avoid additional lawsuits by ceasing production and sales of the drug. In addition to affecting employees' jobs, such a decision would suddenly make less available and perhaps even unavailable a drug that had been used effectively in treating medical problems in parts of the body other than the eye. A reduction in the drug's availability would probably raise the price of the drug for patients who would have to obtain it from other manufacturers. If other American companies were frightened away from producing the drug because of their fear that they could be subject to similar lawsuits, the drug may become prohibitively expensive as people seek to obtain it from foreign manufacturers or it may simply become completely unavailable in the United States. The jury award may cause insurance companies to raise the premiums that they charge to drug manufacturers in order to guard against liability in other lawsuits and drug manufacturers would then raise the prices of all of their products in order to pay for the increased premiums. Insurance companies may also raise the premiums that they charge all customers, including individuals, in order to pay for significant awards in medical tort cases. In sum, the result of a tort case between a single individual and a drug manufacturer may affect everyone in American society by raising the prices for various products and potentially reducing or eliminating the availability of products that may be useful or even necessary in the treatment of specific medical conditions.

For a variety of medical conditions that affect relatively small numbers of people, companies are reluctant to make therapeutic drugs available to the American market. As Peter Huber has described:

> Chemie Grunenthal, for example, a West German company that once supplied thalidomide to American leprosy victims, announced in 1986 it planned to abandon the U.S. market to avoid the risk of liability that might arise if, for example, the drug was used in excess or fell into the wrong hands. Until recently, another West German chemical company supplied Americans with botulinum, a paralytic poison that is just right for controlling eye-twitching disease, but the company cut off supplies in 1986 for similar reasons.[6]

Decisions produced by the courts in tort litigation may have profound policy consequences for society by determining the availability and cost of products and services. These policy-shaping decisions are not planned, but are developed on an *ad hoc* basis in reaction to specific, discrete incidents in which a person suffers an injury. Students of public policy generally learn that policy initiatives are best developed by "the rational decision maker who lays out goals and uses logical processes to explore the best way to reach those goals."[7] The *ad hoc* nature of tort litigation and its attendant policy consequences depart significantly from this ideal of rational policy-making. In tort litigation, there is a risk that the cost and availability of products for all citizens may be affected by isolated or unrepresentative incidents. For example, the aforementioned large monetary award in Chicago for injuries to the man's eye involved an unusual and, according to the defendant pharmaceutical company, improper application of the drug by the treating physician. If the drug is removed from the market as a result of this allegedly improper usage and subsequent jury decision, people who benefitted from proper usage will also be deprived of access.

The *ad hoc* nature of tort litigation is compounded by the fact that most juries may find a drug or other product to be safe, but it may take only one isolated jury to go against the weight of medical evidence to force a product from the market. Huber describes how this process affected one drug for morning-sickness:

> Is Bendectin a safe and valuable morning-sickness therapy, as the [Food and Drug Administration] has concluded, or a terato-genic poison responsible for countless birth defects, as several juries have declared, with a conviction measured in the hundreds of millions of dollars? The mainstream scientific community has agreed with the FDA. So have most juries, but not all, and the courthouse door is always open for the issue to be relitigated anew. Bendectin is off the market as a result.[8]

Despite the fact that decisions are made on a case-by-case basis, civil litigation verdicts are not left completely to the whims of judges and juries in each case. Case decisions are guided, but not necessarily controlled, by the substantive legal rules governing liability (i.e., which parties can be made legally responsible for what kinds of injuries) and the behavior of juries (i.e., how much compensation do jurors believe a particular kind of injury is worth). These factors shape but do not always determine case outcomes because, respectively, judges sometimes change substantive tort law through the common law judicial decision-making process and judges sometimes reduce jury awards. Thus, although juries frequently make the most important decisions in policy-shaping tort litigation, judges can influence and limit jurors' discretion in assessing liability and awarding damages for injuries.

The Development of Substantive Tort Law

Under the common law system that the United States inherited from Great Britain, judges are supposed to examine case precedents in reaching decisions for cases involving similar factual circumstances to those that have arisen in previous cases. The process of legal reasoning in such cases was described by Edward Levi as a three-step process for judges: "[first], similarity is seen between [the case before the judge and prior] cases; next the rule of law inherent in the [most similar prior] case is announced; then the rule of law is made applicable [to the current case before the judge]."[9] By relying on decisions in prior cases, judges need not "start from scratch" in attempting to develop fair legal rules to govern a particular kind of dispute. Reliance upon case precedents also contributes to stability in law and to the equal application of rules to similarly situated individuals. Although there are benefits of efficiency, stability, and equity through reliance on previous case decisions, rigid adherence to precedents creates risks that rules of behavior for a bygone era will continue to control in a society that faces different problems. Thus the common law process creates opportunities for judges to adjust and change case law by examining precedents "in light of the immediate case as well as any new social conditions."[10]

With regard to tort law, as American society became increasingly industrialized and technologically complex, the laws for assigning legal liability and financial responsibility changed. According to Kermit Hall, "tort law shifted from the nineteenth-century concern with fault and blameworthiness to the contemporary stress on compensation of injured persons."[11] This shift in emphasis contributed to the cumulative policy impacts of civil litigation by gradually increasing both the likelihood and extent of compensation for people's injuries. Although American judges bear significant responsibility for changing the orientation of tort law by employing the common law process to gradually change substantive legal rules governing liability, legislatures also contributed to this shift through the enactment of no-fault automobile insurance and other statutory changes emphasizing compensation instead of fault.

In the mid-nineteenth century, "negligence began . . . to be recognized as a separate basis for tort liability, independent of other causes of action. Its rise coincided to a marked degree with the industrial revolution in England."[12] People began to bear financial responsibility for injuries to persons or property caused as a consequence of their failure to behave in a reasonably, prudent manner. According to G. Edward White, "the modern negligence principle in tort law seems to have been an intellectual response to the increased number of accidents involving persons who had no preexisting relationship with one another—'stranger' cases."[13]

American judges' tort decisions in the mid-nineteenth century limited the opportunities for injured workers to recover for their injuries unless they could prove that their employers were at fault. For example, in the 1842 case of *Farwell v. Boston & Worcester Railroad Corp.*,[14] an engineer whose hand was crushed when a co-worker improperly threw a switch was prevented from suing his employer because, according to the judge, the engineer assumed the risk of such an injury by accepting the potentially dangerous railroad job. Moreover, the judge said that the engineer should sue the co-worker responsible for the accident rather than the railroad.[15] The foregoing doctrines, known respectively as "assumption of risk" and the "fellow-servant rule," as well as the doctrine of "contributory negligence," which barred recovery if the victim's conduct contributed to the injury in any small way, emphasized the imposition of liability only for established fault. During the period of industrialization, these rules for negligence cases helped to reduce the financial risks and burdens for developing business enterprises. According to Kermit Hall, "[judges] accepted that some injuries would go uncompensated and that a fault standard . . . would facilitate economic development by insulating entrepreneurs from the costs of accidents."[16] The primary exception to this emphasis on the fault of tort defendants rather than on compensation for injured victims was the courts' solicitude to passengers injured in public transportation accidents on railroads and steamships.[17]

Negligence standards were expanded to apply to manufacturers of products in 1916 in a case concerning a defective wheel on an automobile.[18] Manufacturers were required to take due care in manufacturing products to ensure that purchasers of the products would not be injured. Over time, liability was expanded to cover injuries to non-purchasers (i.e., users, bystanders, etc.) caused by negligently manufactured products. According to Huber, the significant expansion of tort liability for manufacturers occurred during the 1960s when companies became financially responsible not only for injuries caused by *manufacturing defects*, but also for injuries caused by *design defects*:

> Like so many other changes in the tort rules, the step from manufacturing defects to design defects was presented as the soul of modesty. But with that simple change the courts plunged into a new and daunting enterprise. To begin with, the stakes in design defect cases are much higher. A manufacturing-defect verdict condemns only a single item coming off the assembly line. But a defect of design condemns the entire production, and a loss in one case almost inevitably implies losses in many others. Moreover, design is a much more subtle business than manufacture, and identifying deficiencies is vastly more difficult.[19]

The expansion of tort liability for design defects gave jurors, who are non-specialist citizens drawn from the community, the ability to decide that a product should have had an additional safety device or should have been made out of stronger materials. By giving jurors the opportunity to second-guess manufacturers' design decisions, tort law provides the opportunity to emphasize compensation for injured people rather than to follow the earlier legal rules concerning precise determinations of fault. The expansion of liability forces manufacturers to provide a kind of "insurance" for injuries that occur after use of their products, sometimes even when preexisting conditions affecting the victim or misuse of the product are the most direct causes of injuries. Under the compensation emphasis of tort law, lawyers seek to sue entities that possess "deep pockets," such as corporations and other asset-rich or well-insured defendants. Juries respond by requiring larger than usual damages from corporations and insurance companies, whether or not they are most responsible for the injuries, simply because these entities are best able to provide compensation. For example, "Sears lost a $1.2 million judgment to a man who suffered a heart attack caused (he alleged) by a lawn mower rope that was too hard to pull,"[20] and Goodyear and Ford were liable for a driver's death when a tire exploded as he drove more than one hundred miles per hour on tires designed for a maximum safe speed of eighty-five miles per hour.[21] As noted by George Priest:

> [C]ourts justified the expansion of liability to provide victim insurance on two grounds: corporations can obtain insurance more cheaply than victims; and tort law can provide compensation insurance to individuals—chiefly the poor—who may not purchase first-party injury insurance themselves.[22]

In addition to expanding liability for manufacturers, judicial decisions expanded opportunities to file lawsuits against someone for failing to control the conduct of other people. For example, new lawsuits succeeded against mental health professionals (e.g., for violence committed by their patients), employers (e.g., for violence committed by their employees), landlords (e.g., for failing to prevent crimes against their tenants), and cities (e.g., for failing to stop a suicide attempt).[23] Because the people most directly responsible for the foregoing harms are unlikely to be able to compensate their victims (e.g., people incarcerated in mental hospitals or prisons frequently have few assets), the underlying motivation for this expansion of liability seemed to be a search for someone—not necessarily the person most responsible for the injury—who possessed the financial assets or insurance coverage necessary for compensating victims. Thus, substantive tort law moved away from an emphasis on fault and toward an emphasis on compensating people for their injuries.

Damages Awarded in Tort Cases

Juries

Juries decide how much compensation people should receive for injuries to their person or property. Because juries decide how much a victim should receive, the verdict represents a statement from the community about how injuries should be valued. In making their determinations, jurors are inevitably influenced by their attitudes, prejudices, and biases. Individual jurors also have differing capacities for remembering and understanding expert testimony and judges' instructions to the jury.[24] Thus, there is always an element of unpredictability in jury verdicts.

In seeking to improve their chances for success in civil litigation, attorneys use various strategies to influence the composition and decisions of juries. Attorneys may hire "jury experts" who develop demographic profiles to predict what kinds of jurors will be sympathetic.[25] Attorneys use their questioning of jurors and their peremptory challenges to exclude specific individuals in order to seek a jury composed of favorable jurors. For example, a defense attorney in products liability litigation may wish to have people who work in business on the jury because they may sympathize with manufacturers' policies and practices. Jury experts may also supervise mock trials that enable lawyers to test their arguments in front of experimental jurors, citizens hired to serve on a mock jury. When M.C.I. Communications won $1.8 billion in a jury trial against its telephone company rival, American Telephone and Telegraph (AT&T), MCI's success was attributed to its lawyers' practice trials before mock juries, which provided feedback about the persuasiveness of strategic presentations of arguments and evidence.[26] Although there are doubts about the extent to which lawyers can effectively manipulate jury composition and otherwise affect trial outcomes through the use of jury experts,[27] lawyers are still anxious to use any available tactic to improve their chances for success: "When enormous sums of money are at risk so that even a small increase in the probability of one more favorable juror represents a major achievement, cost-benefit analysis may justify the investment in [jury experts] despite the uncertainty [of success]."[28] Underlying the use of attorneys' strategies is one inescapable aspect of civil litigation: it is a very human process with uncertain outcomes that depend upon the opinions and actions of human beings drawn from through-out society.

Compensation for Injuries

Injured plaintiffs who prevail in tort cases are entitled to compensatory damages that are intended to pay them for the value of their losses. Obviously, it is difficult to place a value on the loss of a body part or the death of a child, but citizens drawn from the community are given the responsibility for making such determinations. It becomes even more difficult to assess injuries when jurors are asked to compensate victims for especially intangible harms such as "pain and suffering" or psychological injuries.

Juries sometimes award punitive damages that are designed to punish the wrongdoer and deter future harmful conduct. Jurors have no solid basis for setting punitive damages other than their collective perception about what amount will punish the wrongdoer effectively. As Huber observes, juries have gradually been increasing awards in selected cases and thereby placing greater economic burdens upon tort defendants and the insurance companies with which the defendants have policies:

> Since the early 1960s, average awards have been rising much faster than either medical costs or wages. An estimated 30 to 40 percent of awards in personal injury cases today are attributable to psychic distress of one sort or another, and the fraction is rising steadily. . . . In 1986, an eight-year-old girl left paralyzed and brain-damaged after she fell out of a Jeep won a $23.7 million verdict, including $6 million for pain and suffering. (The jury concluded that the girl's mother was 75 percent responsible in failing to lock the door and to restrain the child with a seat belt, but the award was issued nevertheless.) In July 1986, a New York court awarded $65 million to a Brooklyn woman who lost most of her small intestines when a hospital failed to diagnose an obstruction in her stomach, $58 million of which was for pain and suffering.[29]

Even intangible injuries, such as harm to someone's reputation by slander or libel, can produce large punitive damages. For example, a tabloid magazine was ordered to pay $650,000 in compensatory damages and an additional $850,000 in punitive damage to an elderly woman in Arkansas whose picture was featured in a fictitious article about a "101-year-old Australian newspaper carrier [who] had to quit her route because she had gotten pregnant by a millionaire customer."[30] Although few people have sympathy for a tabloid newspaper that publishes phony stories, such large awards can affect both the publication's insurance company, which will spread the costs among its other insurance customers through higher premiums, and the newspaper's employees if the large award reduces the paper's ability to continue operating.

It is these exceptional, notable cases rather than average cases that have increased the financial pressures upon tort litigation defendants and their insurance companies. A study in Chicago found that "[a]fter having awarded only $1.6 million (in 1984 dollars) during the previous 20 years, Cook County juries awarded $27 million during the 1980s. Most of these dollars were awarded in *three cases* with exceptionally large awards" (emphasis added).[31]

Although significant punitive damages may be assessed in relatively few cases, they can have serious economic consequences for businesses, insurers, and everyone in American society. As James Levine observed:

> Companies can be put on the brink of bankruptcy. The extraordinary $10.53 billion damage award against Texaco for interfering with Pennzoil's attempted purchase of Getty [Oil Co.] put Texaco in a situation in which it was fighting for survival. Many economic interests were at stake: the value of Texaco stock to shareholders, the jobs of Texaco's employees, amounts owed to Texaco's creditors, taxes due from Texaco, and the livelihood of people and businesses in communities where Texaco is a major presence. The jury's verdict threatened the survival of the nation's third-largest oil corporation.[32]

Damages awarded by juries have other effects upon society. Medical malpractice lawsuits, for example, have multiple effects. Not only do doctors pass along to their patients the increasing costs of insurance premiums, but doctors also increase the medical costs to patients (and society) by practicing "defensive medicine."[33] In order to protect themselves against lawsuits, doctors order additional expensive laboratory tests to make sure that they have not missed any information in formulating a diagnosis. Doctors perform unnecessary tonsillectomies, hysterectomies, Caesarian childbirth deliveries, and other procedures that are not warranted by the patient's condition. Instead of diagnosing and treating conditions according to normal medical procedures, doctors are encouraged to employ additional expensive tests, surgical procedures, and drugs on all patients to guard against the potential lawsuits by the small percentage of patients whose conditions may not improve from the usual treatment methods.

Jury awards also serve to create local standards for settlement discussions in civil litigation. Most civil lawsuits are resolved through negotiated settlements rather than through trials. Out of the 2,835,491 civil case dispositions in state courts during 1988, only 9.2 percent of these cases led to a trial. Moreover, juries participated in fewer than 13 percent of the civil trials;[34] most trials were "bench trials" in which a judge was the decision maker. The small number of cases in which juries make decisions serve to provide the basis for attorneys' negotiations in the 90 percent of cases that never reach the trial stage. If juries in a particular city tend to award $50,000 for a particular kind of injury in an automobile accident, lawyers for injured plaintiffs and the insurance companies that usually represent defendants will base their settlement negotiations upon their expectations about how a jury would decide the case if it went to trial. Thus jury awards determine the outcomes and consequences of tort lawsuits, even in cases that never reach the trial stage of the judicial process.

For example, when an errant police bullet went through the wall of a house in Barberton, Ohio and killed an innocent homeowner sleeping inside, the city's agreement to settle any potential lawsuit for the man's death by paying the family $1.2 million was not based upon the city's altruistic evaluation concerning how much money they ought to pay for causing the death. The amount was determined through an assessment by the city's attorney about how much a jury might award if the case were to go to trial. In fact, the Barberton city attorney's letter to the city council concerning the settlement justified the amount by specifically discussing the likely jury award in a trial.[35] By assessing the potential jury award and arriving at a negotiated settlement, the city—or any other defendant—can resolve their potential liability while avoiding the significant litigation expenses (e.g., attorneys' fees, court costs, discovery costs, etc.) that would be incurred if the case were to proceed through the entire judicial process.

Questioning the Extent of the Litigation "Crisis"

The expansion and attendant societal impact of tort lawsuits and other civil litigation cases are purported to be components of a "litigation explosion" afflicting American court systems. Because, in Lawrence Friedman's characterization, Americans seek "total justice" when they perceive that they have been wronged, they are quick to use the judicial process to pursue grievances.[36] Many commentators have claimed that the United States has abnormally high litigation rates that unnecessarily clog American courts with cases and expend excessive societal resources on attorneys' fees, court costs, and the other expenses associated with civil litigation.[37] Because the United States has more lawyers (estimated to be 750,000 in 1990) and more lawyers per capita (1 lawyer per 360 people) than virtually any other country in the world[38] and because lawyers profit from litigation, lawyers supposedly encourage Americans to initiate expensive and time-consuming litigation, even for claims of questionable validity. As one national news magazine glibly observed: "Fish gotta swim. Locusts devour the countryside. Lawyers sue [and thereby cause] . . . the American plague of overlitigation."[39] Thus the American cultural inclination to litigate disputes and the overabundance of self-interested lawyers are believed to exacerbate the cumulative effects that civil litigation has upon public policy in the United States.

Although it is clear that civil litigation affects public policy, it is difficult to assess the extent to which litigation shapes policy development and the distribution of resources throughout society. As with most discussions of tort litigation and high damage awards, the foregoing discussion in this chapter cited several eye-catching cases in which people won large sums of money with attendant economic consequences for society. Examples of "big" cases attract attention but do not present a complete portrait of litigation. The news article's headline announces, for example, that "Confessed Mass-Slayer Dahmer Sued for $3 Billion by Missing Man's Kin,"[40] but will the newspaper later report the inevitable conclusion to the case when the victims' relatives are unable to obtain a single cent from the unskilled chocolate factory worker who murdered people in his dilapidated apartment? While it is true that there are numerous examples of large settlements and jury awards in tort cases, news reports on these cases often distort the public's perception of civil litigation and thus the policy consequences of litigation may be exaggerated. Any time one relies upon *anecdotal evidence* (i.e., examples of specific cases) instead of *systematic empirical evidence* (i.e., systematic studies of large numbers of cases), there is a risk that conclusions may be inaccurate and distorted. For example, although people frequently cite large jury awards to argue that juries have gone too far in redistributing resources in society, empirical studies of jury awards indicate that most jury awards are relatively modest. Although the largest jury awards—the ones that attract attention from the media and the public—have grown larger, most damage awards and settlements have not changed drastically. A well-known study of jury verdicts in Cook County, Illinois (i.e., Chicago and surrounding area) from 1960 to 1980 found that "[f]or most injuries and most case types, juries awarded almost identical compensation in the two decades, after adjusting for inflation."[41] Other studies indicate that the true cost of jury awards may be exaggerated because judges sometimes reduce juries' awards to plaintiffs. Thus one study found that after reductions of excessive awards by judges, defendants actually had to pay only 71 percent of the total damages that the juries had originally awarded.[42]

In addition, other studies indicate that the litigation rate in the United States is not uniquely high but is comparable to that in many other industrialized countries.[43] Although Americans are supposedly "the most litigious people on the globe,"[44] Americans do not necessarily file lawsuits whenever they are harmed. For example, a study of 31,000 randomly selected hospital records in New York found that out of the 280 patients who suffered "adverse events caused by medical negligence," fewer than 2 percent filed malpractice suits.[45] People may not recognize that they have a legally compensable injury or they may be deterred from filing lawsuits by the financial expenses and psychological costs of initiating litigation. Many potential claims are never pursued and others are dropped when people no longer have the patience, will, or resources to continue through the expensive, time-consuming process of civil litigation.[46]

Even if one concludes that there is too much litigation in the United States, other critics argue that this represents a problem of too many injuries being caused by defective products, unsafe workplaces, and other correctable conditions caused by business and government.[47] According to the viewpoint of these critics, "civil litigation is only beginning to correspond to widespread grievances heretofore not heard in our troubled society."[48] If this is true (and it is the subject of debate), then policymakers' concerns should be directed at preventing the human suffering that generates litigation rather than at altering the litigation process itself.

The causes of the adverse policy consequences of civil litigation have also been questioned. For example, although the threat of malpractice lawsuits is purported to encourage doctors to increase the expense of treatment by practicing "defensive medicine," doctors also have their own self-interest in such practices. Although doctors may claim that they do extra tests, do more surgical procedures than doctors in other countries, and use expensive high-tech equipment in order to guard against lawsuits, these procedures also add to the doctors' profits by permitting them to pad bills with extra charges for the patients (and the patients' insurance companies).[49] What creates the adverse policy consequences of spiraling medical costs, the threat of litigation or doctors' financial self-interest? Undoubtedly both factors are at work, but it is difficult to know which factor is more influential.

Similarly, many cities, day care centers, and other entities have had difficulty obtaining liability insurance because the price of insurance premiums has risen rapidly and some companies will no longer insure certain enterprises and activities that may generate litigation. Although insurance companies assert that the pressures of civil litigation have forced them to raise rates and reduce coverage, critics contend that the insurance companies have remained profitable despite their claims of hardship. These critics claim that the companies may be merely generating publicity about a supposed litigation "crisis" in order to persuade legislators to limit opportunities for tort victims to obtain damage awards—and thereby further increase the financial profitability of the insurance industry.[50]

Political Reactions to Perceptions About Litigation

Whether or not the causes, nature, and extent of civil litigation can be accurately assessed, it is clear that such litigation produces cumulative policy consequences for society by distributing resources and shaping rules for behavior (e.g., how products must be designed, etc.). More importantly, the perceived policy consequences of civil litigation have generated political reactions by actors who believe (or claim to believe) that litigation adversely affects them and by other political interests that view court reform as a means to attain political or economic advantages.

In 1991, after the composition of the U.S. Supreme Court had become more conservative through appointments by Presidents Reagan and Bush, eighty corporate and insurance organizations filed legal briefs supporting an insurance company's efforts to obtain a judicially-created cap on punitive damages in tort cases.[51] A poor woman found herself stuck with $3,500 in medical bills after her insurance agent pocketed her insurance premiums rather than submitting them to the company in order to maintain her policy's medical coverage. A jury found the agent's employer, Pacific Mutual Life Insurance Company, liable for his actions and awarded the woman $1 million, including $840,000 in punitive damages.[52] The company argued to the Supreme Court that excessive jury awards violate the Constitution's Fourteenth Amendment Due Process Clause. The justices rejected the company's claims by a seven to one vote and declined to create any rules about what constitutes acceptable damage awards.[53] Although the advocates of tort law reform have failed to obtain judicial policies to limit jury awards, they have found more receptive audiences in the legislative and executive branches of government.

The insurance industry has maintained a steady public relations campaign designed to pressure elected officials and judges to reduce the scope of tort liability and limit the payment of damage awards. For example, a two-page advertisement placed in *Time* magazine by an international insurance organization sought to inform the public about the economic costs that tort litigation imposes upon American society:

> In reality, the American system of liability has become the source of a hidden tax on our economy—a tax that can account for as much as 50% of the price paid for a product.
> What's worse, it has been estimated that this hidden tax amounts to $80 billion a year—a sum equal to the combined profits of the nation's 200 largest corporations.
> Our economic competitors' legal systems do not encourage litigation to the extent we do. Consider, for example, that there are 30 times more lawsuits per capita in the U.S. than in Japan. Is it any wonder that America is having a tough time competing in overseas markets? [54]

By characterizing the problem as one that adversely affects the American economy rather than as a self-interested issue for the insurance industry, the advocates of tort reform seek to appeal to a broad spectrum of society. In 1991, the Bush administration seized upon the issue as an organizing focus for domestic policy proposals. President Bush's first initiative for improving the nation's health care system was limited to a proposal to place caps on damage awards in medical malpractice cases. [55] Vice President Quayle's Council for Competitiveness proposed a variety of court reforms, including limitations on punitive damages, as the means to increase the financial viability and economic competitiveness of American corporations. [56] Although these proposals addressed aspects of the cumulative policy consequences from civil litigation, these initiatives were also tailored to gain partisan political advantages for Republicans. The Council's activities in diluting environmental regulations and other legal restraints on corporations gave it a reputation as a semi-secret agency working to provide advantages for a primary Republican business constituency. As characterized by one national news magazine, "[f]or industries trying to skirt the law, Dan Quayle's Council on Competitiveness is a good place to start." [57] By Executive Order, President Bush implemented some of the Council's recommendations for changing procedures in federal courts. [58] Because the Bush administration was frequently criticized for failing to pursue policy initiatives to address such problems as health care and the economic recession,[59] court reform proposals provide, from a politician's perspective, a cost-free mechanism for appearing to take action on domestic issues. If enacted, these proposals would have only modest effects on the larger issues of the availability of health care and the nation's economic problems, but they would not require any increases in taxes or governmental expenditures. In addition, the Bush administration could portray itself as fighting against the unpopular interest group that most actively opposes tort reform, American lawyers.

It is difficult to say which reforms will be enacted at the federal level. Because there is no consensus on the precise causes and extent of the adverse consequences of civil litigation, any reforms that are implemented will be the product of competitive interactions between competing political interests. It is unclear whether the business interests and insurance organizations that advocate tort reform can effectively persuade Congress to enact reform legislation when other interests, primarily lawyers' organizations and consumer advocates, are strongly opposed to limitations upon damage awards.

At the state level, legislatures in several states have enacted tort reform statutes to limit damage awards. For example, New Hampshire abolished punitive damages and Oklahoma, Colorado, and Florida created ceilings on punitive damage awards by linking such awards to the amount of compensatory damages.[60] Ohio's legislature sought to remove from juries their authority to determine punitive damages and place that power in the hands of trial judges who, presumably, will be less inclined to make large awards.[61] Because powerful organized interests are at odds over the desirability of tort reform, it is unclear whether sufficient political momentum will develop to lead state legislators to limit the power of juries. Although such actions would reduce the economic consequences of litigation for society by inhibiting juries from spreading the cost of injuries among businesses, insurance companies, and their customers, tort reform also can diminish the "democratic" element in civil litigation, namely citizen participation in judicial decision making. As John Stookey argues:

> If we think about twentieth century tort law issues, they relate to political attempts to limit or broaden the power and authority of lay participants. For example, workers compensation took away the right of injured workers to use the legal system. It simultaneously took away the jury's right to determine the appropriate value for a worker injury. Current no fault [insurance] plans and limits on damages are of the same type. The political message

seems to be that citizen participants in the legal system cannot be trusted to act for the common good.[62]

Conclusion

Because of the complex causes and diffuse, cumulative consequences of civil litigation, it is difficult to define precisely the nature and extent of litigation's impact on public policy. It is clear that civil litigation, particularly tort lawsuits, generates consequences that affect everyone in American society. The cost and availability of products and services are determined by both trends in jury verdicts and the settlement negotiations in untried cases that are influenced by those verdicts. Although interest groups and politicians have pressured legislators, with modest success at the state level, to create statutory limitations on damage awards, there is a continuing debate among competing political interests about whether such limitations actually benefit society or if they merely protect business interests at the expense of injured individuals.

CHAPTER 9
JUDICIAL POLICY-MAKING: A CONCLUDING NOTE

SHOULD JUDGES MAKE PUBLIC policy decisions for the United States? When they do, how is American society affected by decisions emanating from courts rather than from legislative or executive governmental institutions? These are the important and controversial questions that will continue to be at the center of perpetual debates among scholars, social commentators, and public officials. Although scholars accurately note that it is obvious "[t]hat the Supreme Court [and other courts have] always acted as . . . policy-making [institutions],"[1] critics, such as William H. Rehnquist, Chief Justice of the United States, argue that judges "were not appointed to roam at large in the realm of public policy."[2] When judges make public policy decisions, there are risks that they are exceeding the power granted to them under the United States Constitution. Moreover, other institutions and decision makers may be more capable of making good public policy decisions that will achieve intended goals without producing undesirable consequences. Yet as indicated by the preceding chapters, there is reason to dispute categorical denunciations of judicial policy-making as improper and undesirable.

The Future of Judicial Policy-Making

Some might argue that such controversies will diminish during the 1990s as the predominantly conservative federal judiciary reduces its

143

involvement with the policy issues that captured judicial attention during the 1960s, 1970s, and 1980s. From this perspective, as conservative advocates of "judicial restraint" don black robes and become the authoritative decision makers within the judicial branch, they may withdraw the courts from the policy controversies that were discussed in the preceding chapters. If judicial policy-making is exclusively associated with politically liberal judges, then presumably conservative judges will restore the courts to their "true" role and no longer engage in policy-making. In fact, however, judicial policy-making is not associated with any particular political ideology.

The phrase "judicial policy-making" is frequently applied to situations in which judges' decisions clash with, fail to defer to, or preempt decisions by other branches of government. From the 1950s to the 1980s, those clashes frequently pitted the decisions of liberal federal judges against the more conservative inclinations of Congress, the President, and state government officials. In earlier periods of American history, however, when conservative judicial officers clashed with more liberal elected officials, it was the conservatives who were "judicial activists" engaged in policy-making. Most notably, during the first four decades of the twentieth century, conservative justices on the U.S. Supreme Court overrode the will of the state legislatures, Congress, and the President by invalidating economic regulation and social welfare statutes designed to address specific modern social problems. During that era, according to Chief Justice Rehnquist, "the Court was dealing body blows to . . . state and federal legislation that arose out of the Progressive movement."[3] Ultimately, the Court backed down in the face of threats to its structural integrity when President Franklin Roosevelt proposed expanding the size of the Court in order to neutralize the activist conservatives through the appointment of additional liberal justices. Shortly thereafter, the aging conservatives began to retire and Roosevelt replaced them with his supporters.[4] Thus, the Supreme Court's political composition caught up with the liberalizing trends that had already affected the voters' choices for elected officials.

The newly dominant conservative justices on the Supreme Court during the late 1980s and early 1990s showed similar inclinations to become activist policy-makers when confronted with liberal legislation with which they disagreed.[5] For example, in 1989 the conservative justices rewrote the meaning of statutory interpretation precedents that had existed for eighteen[6] and thirteen years,[7] respectively, in order to make it more difficult for people to initiate lawsuits alleging employment discrimination. Both of these decisions were subsequently reversed by corrective legislation from Congress.[8] During the same year, when the Supreme Court's conservative majority invalidated the City of Richmond's affirmative action program for ensuring that a portion of public contract funds went to minority-owned businesses,[9] the justices' action reshaped public policy in contravention of a policy choice enacted by the duly elected representatives of the citizens of Richmond. Were these legitimate judicial actions? Were they consistent with the appropriate constitutional role for the judiciary?

In the employment discrimination example, the Court replaced the decisions of accountable, elected policymakers (i.e., members of Congress) with its own views about how employment discrimination cases should be pursued. In the example of the affirmative action program, the conservative justices used their responsibility for upholding individuals' rights under the Constitution, specifically white business owners' right to Equal Protection, as the justification for supplanting the policy judgments of elected officials. These were precisely the kinds of actions (albeit not as intrusive as liberal judges' prison reform and school desegregation decisions) that angered political conservatives in the 1960s and 1970s about the policy-making actions of liberal judges whose decisions overrode the policy choices of legislative and executive branch officials. Although people may agree or disagree with the propriety of the conservative justices' actions, just as they argue about the actions of liberal judicial officers in previous decades, these cases demonstrate that judicial policy-making is not the exclusive domain of judicial officers who possess any particular ideology. Liberal and conservative judges both engage in policy-making. Judicial influence over public policy is inevitable in a system with authoritative judges who are the products of political processes and who, as guardians of the Constitution, are available to hear claims from the public.

Dominance of the judiciary by conservative judicial officers will reshape the courts' policy influence over specific issues. For example, conservatives are likely to be more concerned with property rights than with rights for criminal defendants. Thus, a shift in the ideological orientation of judicial decision makers alters but does not necessarily reduce or eliminate judicial policy-making.

There is every reason to continue the ongoing debates about the legitimacy and capacity of judicial policy making *in specific cases*, but, as a general matter, it would be naive to assert that American society can simply decide whether there will or will not be judicial policy-making. The American constitutional system empowers the judicial branch as an authoritative decision-making institution. Judges' decisions inevitably create rules for behavior. Judges' decisions inevitably determine the allocation of benefits and burdens. Judges' decisions inevitably clash, at least sometimes, with the policy preferences implemented by legislative and executive branch officials. In sum, judicial policy-making is an inevitable component of the American governing system. Judicial influence over public policy shall continue in various forms as long as the United States maintains its current governmental institutions. Thus, rather than debate a hypothetical question concerning American political theory (i.e., "Does the Constitution authorize judicial policy-making?"), the most pressing issues confronting interested observers concern how an important, visible, and inevitable phenomenon, namely judicial policy-making, should be evaluated.

Politics and Complexity

Two notable observations emerge from the examples presented in the preceding chapters about the processes and consequences of judicial impacts upon public policy. First, the courts' *intimate connections to the political system* both shape and limit judicial impacts upon public policy. There are numerous examples of political aspects of the judicial process. Interest groups and individual litigants, motivated by political self-interest, help to set the courts' agenda by initiating and pursuing cases that raise issues with public policy implications. The courts are regarded by both conservatives and liberals as just another branch of government that is available for the presentation of specially-tailored policy initiatives. Although decision making within the judicial branch is constrained by the permissible forms for claimants' arguments, other aspects of judicial decision making resemble policy-making processes in other branches of government. As in the legislative and executive branches of government, the substantive content of judicial decisions is shaped by the attitudes, values, and policy preferences of decision makers drawn from the political process. Because courts have limited ability to ensure that judicial policy decisions are implemented, the effectiveness of judicial decisions hinges upon the reactions of other actors and institutions in the political system.

Second, the policy-making process in the judicial branch involves *complex interactions* between litigants, judges, and external political actors. The stereotypical image of powerful judges making straightforward decisions after hearing evidence from two adversarial parties does not capture the essence of policy-making cases. Decisions are developed through strategic interactions and negotiations during the litigation process. Actual policy outcomes are determined by judicial interaction with executive branch officials who must enforce court decisions, legislatures that must respond to those decisions, and citizens who are expected to obey judicial directives. Because the public and the other governmental branches do not necessarily follow judges' decisions, the actual policy outcomes that affect people's lives may not achieve the judges' original objectives. Court decisions do not settle policy issues, but instead frequently generate ongoing policy battles between various political interests.

In contrast to the competing and sometimes one-dimensional arguments asserted by critics and supporters of judicial involvement in public policy, a different picture emerges upon recognition of the political aspects and complexity of judicial policy-making. Judges are actually less powerful policymakers than they are portrayed by critics who fear dictatorial judicial action. In addition, courts cannot fulfill their supporters' image as effective forums for policy-making. The myriad political constraints on judicial power and the complex nature of judicial policy-making limit the effectiveness of courts as policy-making institutions.

Assessing the Policy-Making Role of Courts

If courts are neither as powerful nor as effective as they are purported to be, what conclusions can be drawn about the policy-making role of American courts? There is no escaping the fact that courts help to shape public policy in important ways through directed actions by judges, negotiations by litigants, reactions by external political actors, and the cumulative processes of civil litigation. Thus, although courts do not necessarily dictate or determine public policy outcomes, judicial processes influence public policy by contributing to ongoing interactions among political interests, governing institutions, and other policy-shaping actors within the political system. Judicial processes and decisions may help to set the policy agendas for the other governmental branches that are more effective in initiating *and* implementing public policy decisions. The reactions of legislators or executive branch officials may ultimately be more influential in defining public policy, but courts play a role in pushing governmental institutions to take action. Judicial actions may also mobilize individuals and interest groups to lobby legislatures, generate electoral activity, file new legal cases, and otherwise devote resources and energy toward the advancement of policy preferences. Thus, traditional democratic political processes continue to exert significant influence over policy decisions by government. The courts often merely play a role in defining issues for and motivating action by the political interests whose strategic actions influence policy outcomes.

Judicial Impotence and the Image of Policy-Making

The foregoing characterization of courts as mere influential "participants" in the policy process may strike some observers as an undervaluation and, indeed, even a denigration of the important role that the judicial branch is regarded as playing in determining policy outcomes for civil rights and other policy issues. If courts are merely "participants" rather than "determiners" of public policy, then how would American society and its public policies be different if courts had not been actively involved in policy-making? Were the courts not instrumental in breaking down the discriminatory barriers of racial segregation that oppressed African-Americans? Were the courts not instrumental in recognizing and combatting discrimination against women? Were the courts not instrumental in curbing abusive law enforcement practices by recognizing constitutional rights for criminal defendants and thereby effectively creating rules for proper behavior by law enforcement officials? The answer to these questions and to similar questions that could be posed concerning the importance and consequences of judicial policy-making is a less-than-resounding "maybe."

Courts were instrumental in shaping and changing the aforementioned public policies. Yet in each instance, the judicial declarations emanating from courts were ineffective until they were supported and implemented by legislative and executive branch actions. In his systematic study of courts' impact upon significant social change in American society, Gerald Rosenberg documents the ineffectiveness of judicial action.[10] For example, data on school desegregation indicate that judicial declarations had little effect until Congress and the U.S. Department of Health, Education, and Welfare took active steps to encourage and coerce school systems into compliance during the 1960s.[11] Moreover, Rosenberg questions the Supreme Court's purported indirect impact upon social change by supposedly encouraging civil rights activists through their knowledge that one branch of government recognized and supported the legitimacy of their struggle. Rosenberg found no evidence of increased civil rights activism in the aftermath of Supreme Court decisions. In addition, public opinion polls indicated that many people interested in civil rights were only dimly aware of the judicial decisions in their favor.[12] Rosenberg's thorough examination of empirical evidence on the courts' effects upon abortion, women's rights, environmental issues, and criminal justice policies found a similar dearth of evidence to demonstrate direct or indirect judicial impact on significant social change.

This is not to say that courts did not affect public policy in specific cities and states. However, although school systems within specific cities complied promptly with judicial desegregation orders, national desegregation trends are associated with actions by the legislative and executive branches rather than those of the courts. Rosenberg posits that larger social and economic forces affecting American society turned the United States against official policies of racial discrimination and that the courts were merely participants in processes of social change that would have taken place eventually without any judicial action.[13]

If Rosenberg is correct and, indeed, his systematic evidence merely provides dramatic, concrete support for general findings by others about the relative ineffectiveness of the courts in implementing judicial policy declarations,[14] should analysts conclude that judicial policy-making is fundamentally irrelevant? Rosenberg would carry this reasoning even further by declaring that the United States has "fly-paper court[s]."[15] According to his analysis, American courts capture the attention of political interests who have faith in the efficacy of judicial policy-making and who therefore expend time, energy, money, and other resources on the judicial process that would be better spent on policy-influencing tactics directed at other, more effective governing institutions.[16]

Fundamentally, this is a potentially troubling characterization. Instead of criticizing negative aspects of judicial policy-making by focusing upon the undesirable actions undertaken by presumably powerful courts, this characterization criticizes judicial policy-making for draining away valuable political resources into ineffective and perhaps even irrelevant activities. In sum, the judicial process appears to be a diversionary illusion rather than a forum for authoritative policy-making action.

Modest Expectations and a Functional Role

Lest the foregoing discussion imply that courts are indeed irrelevant, it is useful to keep Rosenberg's study in perspective. Rosenberg's study, which illuminates the relative impotence of courts as policy-makers, focused only upon the question of whether judicial action caused "*significant* social reform" (emphasis in original) or 'policy change with nationwide impact."[17] Viewed from that perspective, courts may very well be lesser spokes in the larger wheel of social forces that moves and changes society. This does not mean, however, that courts have no important impact. As demonstrated by the previous discussions of illustrative policy issues, judicial actions clearly shape and influence public policy developments through the courts' interactions with other political actors and through political reactions to judicial decisions. Judicial declarations determine policy outcomes in specific cases. Judicial processes affect the decisions, actions, and reactions of other policy-making actors. By seeing beyond the courts' image as a powerful policy-making institution, the examples contained in the earlier chapters and the conclusions of Rosenberg's study are not in conflict. They merely indicate that expert commentators as well as the American public must moderate their expectations for the policy-making abilities of the judicial branch. Judicial actions influence public policy, but courts lack the power to finalize policy outcomes and therefore the judiciary cannot determine the course of social change.

Although courts are less powerful than commonly presumed, this does not mean that they are unimportant for American society. Underlying the debates about courts' proper constitutional authority and about judicial policy-making are larger issues concerning courts' functions for society. Even if significant social changes may occur without judicial action, an absence of judicial forums for presentation of policy issues might generate unanticipated adverse consequences for society. In the case of racial discrimination, for example, if courts were unavailable as forums for airing the issue of segregation, would African-Americans have directed greater energy toward the legislative and executive branches which, until the 1960s, were essentially unresponsive to claims about racial discrimination? Would they have patiently waited for the results of the significant, gradual, and largely unrecognized social and economic forces that Rosenberg posits eventually led to social change? Or, would they have revolted? Litigants' beliefs in courts' image as neutral, legal institutions that possess the power to direct public policy may help to preserve order in American society. Courts can provide a focal point for optimistic policy advocacy while the wheel of social change grinds slowly forward. Judicial scholars are accustomed to recognizing the importance of courts as outlets for public dissatisfaction. Courts can channel conflict into dispute-processing forms that do not threaten the social order.[18] Courts facilitate structured argumentation instead of chaotic violence. In societies that lack the promise of constitutional rights and available forums for the presentation of grievances, disaffected political minorities may reach for guns rather than formulate legal arguments. The availability of the judicial process for the presentation of claims may permit public dialogues about policy issues to be maintained until court actions or other events can help to place those issues on the agendas of other policy-making institutions.

It is difficult to prove whether and to what degree courts function as "steam valves" that diminish the risk of revolts and other forms of social disorder. In assessing the role of courts within American society, however, the recognition that courts are less powerful than expected as policy-making institutions should not imply that courts are unimportant. Courts *are* important as participants and contributors to the governing system's policy-making process and, moreover, they may have even greater value outside of the policy-making realm by performing essential underlying functions for the stability of American society.

NOTES

Chapter 1: Courts and Public Policy

1. Thomas R. Dye, *Understanding Public Policy* (Englewood Cliffs, NJ: Prentice-Hall, 1972), p. 1.

2. See Peter Bachrach and Martin Baratz, "Decisions and Non-Decisions," *American Political Science Review*, 57 (1963): 632–42.

3. Deborah Mesce, "More Americans Going Without Health Insurance," *Akron Beacon Journal*, Dec. 19, 1991, p. A6.

4. John W. Kingdon, *Agendas, Alternatives, and Public Policies* (Boston: Little Brown, 1984), p. 3.

5. Lynn Mather, "Policy Making in State Trial Courts," in *The American Courts: A Critical Assessment*, John B. Gates and Charles A. Johnson, eds. (Washington, DC: Congressional Quarterly, 1991), p. 123.

6. Robert H. Bork, *The Tempting of America: The Political Seduction of the Law* (New York: Simon and Schuster, 1990), p. 348.

7. Lawrence Baum, *American Courts: Process & Policy*, 2nd ed. (Boston: Houghton Mifflin, 1990), p. 7.

8. See Mather, "Policy Making in State Trial Courts," pp. 119–57.

9. See Robert A. Carp and C.K. Rowland, *Policymaking and Politics in the Federal District Courts* (Knoxville, TN: University of Tennessee Press, 1983).

10. See Mary Cornelia Porter and G. Alan Tarr, eds., *State Supreme Courts: Policymakers in the Federal System* (Westport, CT: Greenwood Press, 1982).

11. Judy Daubenmier, "Ban on Abortion Aid Killed," *Akron Beacon Journal*, Feb. 21, 1991, p. A7.

12. Sue Davis and Donald R. Songer, "The Changing Role of the United States Court of Appeals: The Flow of Litigation Revisited," *The Justice System Journal*, 13 (1988–1989): 339.

13. See United States Constitution, Article I, Section 8.

14. Ibid.

15. United States Constitution, Article II, Section 2.

16. See *The Prize Cases,* 67 U.S. 635 (1863).

17. United States Constitution, Article II, Section 2.

18. *Marbury v. Madison,* 5 U.S. 137 (1803).

19. See *Dred Scott v. Sanford,* 60 U.S. 393 (1856).

20. See *Lochner v. New York,* 198 U.S. 45 (1905); *Hammer v. Dagenhart,* 247 U.S. 251 (1918).

21. See *Brown v. Board of Education,* 347 U.S. 483 (1954).

22. See *Cohen v. California,* 403 U.S. 15 (1971).

23. See *Mapp v. Ohio,* 367 U.S. 643 (1961).

24. Linda Greenhouse, "High Court Justices Face An Issue Close to Home," *New York Times,* Dec. 13, 1990, p. A20.

25. Ibid.

26. *Gregory and Nugent v. Ashcroft,* 59 U.S.L.W. 4714 (1991).

27. See Christopher E. Smith, "Educating the Public About Courts and Law," *Judicature,* 75 (1991): 109–13.

28. Bork, *The Tempting of America: The Political Seduction of Law,* title page.

29. See Baum, *American Courts: Process and Policy,* pp. 97–168.

30. William H. Rehnquist, *The Supreme Court: How It Was, How It Is* (New York: William Morrow, 1987), p. 291.

31. Joel B. Grossman and Austin Sarat, "Access to Justice and the Limits of Law," *Law and Policy Quarterly,* 3 (1981): 131.

32. See Jesse Kornbluth, "The Woman Who Beat the Klan," in *The Ku Klux Klan: A History of Racism and Violence,* 3rd ed. (Montgomery, AL: Southern Poverty Law Center, 1988), pp. 30–31.

33. Ron Hutcheson, "Free Speech Costs Bundles in Court," *Akron Beacon Journal,* Nov. 11, 1990, p. A7.

34. See Lee Epstein, *Conservatives in Court* (Knoxville, TN: University of Tennessee Press, 1985).

35. See Clement E. Vose, *Caucasians Only* (Berkeley, CA: University of California Press, 1959); Richard Kluger, *Simple Justice: A History of* Brown v. Board of Education *and Black America's Struggle for Equality* (New York: Random House, 1975).

36. Epstein, *Conservatives in Court,* pp. 16–44.

37. Ibid., p. 148.

38. See Karen O'Connor, *Women's Organizations' Use of the Courts* (Lexington, MA: Lexington Books, 1980), pp. 16–28.

39. Epstein, *Conservatives in Court,* pp. 25–27.

40. *Hammer v. Dagenhart,* 247 U.S. 251 (1918).

41. Stephen L. Wasby, "Civil Rights Litigation By Organizations: Constraints and Choices," *Judicature,* 68 (1985): 337–52.

42. Lee Epstein, "Courts and Interest Groups," in *The American Courts: A Critical Assessment*, eds. John B. Gates and Charles A. Johnson (Washington, DC: Congressional Quarterly Press, 1991), pp. 351.

43. Ibid., pp. 345–49.

44. *Kelly, Commissioner, Suffolk County Police Department v. Johnson*, 425 U.S. 238 (1976). See also *Willingham v. Macon Telegraph Publishing Co.*, 507 F.2d 1084 (5th Cir. 1975) (en banc).

45. Stephen Labaton, "Court Rethinking Rule Intended to Slow Frivolous Lawsuits," *New York Times*, Sept. 14, 1990, p. B18.

46. Harry P. Stumpf, *American Judicial Politics* (New York: Harcourt Brace Jovanovich, 1988), p. 42.

47. See Christopher E. Smith, "Polarization and Change in the Federal Courts: *En Banc* Decisions in the U.S. Courts of Appeals," *Judicature*, 74 (1990): 133–37.

48. See C. Neal Tate, "Personal Attribute Models of the Voting Behavior of U.S. Supreme Court Justices: Liberalism in Civil Liberties and Economics Decisions, 1946–1978," *American Political Science Review*, 75 (1981): 355–67.

49. Baum, *American Courts: Process & Policy*, pp. 299–300.

50. Ibid.

51. Bruce J. Biddle, *Role Theory* (New York: Academic Press, 1979), p. 56.

52. Joel B. Grossman, "Role Playing and the Analysis of Judicial Behavior: The Case of Mr. Justice Frankfurter," *Journal of Public Law*, 11 (1962): 294.

53. James L. Gibson, "The Role Concept in Judicial Research," *Law and Policy Quarterly*, 3 (1981): 303.

54. John T. Wold, "Political Orientations, Social Backgrounds, and Role Perceptions of State Supreme Court Judges," *Western Political Quarterly*, 27 (1974): 239–48.

55. James L. Gibson, "Judges' Role Orientations, Attitudes and Decisions: An Interactive Model," *American Political Science Review*, 72 (1978): 911–24.

56. See J. Woodford Howard, *Courts of Appeals in the Federal Judicial System* (Princeton, NJ: Princeton University Press, 1981).

57. Grossman, "Role Playing and the Analysis of Judicial Behavior," pp. 285–309.

58. J. Woodford Howard, "Role Perceptions and Behavior in Three U.S. Courts of Appeals," *Journal of Politics*, 39 (1977): 916–38.

59. Ibid., p. 920.

60. Ibid.

61. *Plyler v. Doe*, 457 U.S. 202, 242 (1982) (Burger, C.J., dissenting).

62. Ibid.

63. Howard, "Role Perceptions and Behavior," p. 921.

64. James L. Gibson, "From Simplicity to Complexity: The Development of Theory in the Study of Judicial Behavior," *Political Behavior*, 5 (1983): 9.

Chapter 2: The Legitimacy of Courts as Policy-Making Forums

1. U.S. Constitution, Article III, Section 1.

2. Alexander Hamilton, "The Federalist, No. 78," in *Courts, Judges, and Politics*, 4th ed., eds. Walter F. Murphy and C. Herman Pritchett (New York: Random House, 1986), p. 15.

3. Ibid., p. 16.

4. *Reynolds v. Sims*, 377 U.S. 533 (1964) (Harlan, J., dissenting).

5. Neil A. Lewis, "Nominee's Replies on Court's Role Bring Questions," *New York Times*, Sept. 18, 1990, p. B7.

6. Christopher Wolfe, *Judicial Activism: Bulwark of Freedom or Precarious Security?* (Pacific Grove, CA: Brooks/Cole, 1991), p. 109.

7. See Howard L. Reiter, *Parties and Elections in Corporate America* (New York: St. Martin's Press, 1987), pp. 203–209.

8. A. Lee Fritschler, *Smoking and Politics: Policymaking and the Federal Bureaucracy*, 3rd ed. (Englewood Cliffs, NJ: Prentice-Hall, 1983), pp. 30–31.

9. *Ruffin v. Commonwealth*, 62 Va. 790, 796 (1871).

10. See David Adamany, "Legitimacy, Realigning Elections, and the Supreme Court," *Wisconsin Law Review*, (1983): 790–846.

11. See Harry P. Stumpf, *American Judicial Politics* (San Diego, CA: Harcourt Brace Jovanovich, 1988), pp. 157–78.

12. Ibid.

13. Lawrence Baum, *American Courts: Process and Policy*, 2nd ed. (Boston: Houghton Mifflin, 1990), pp. 297–300.

14. See J. Woodford Howard, *Courts of Appeals in the Federal Judicial System* (Princeton, NJ: Princeton University Press, 1981).

15. Edwin Meese, "The Battle for the Constitution," *Policy Review*, (1986): 32–35.

16. See Stephen Macedo, *The New Right v. The Constitution* (Washington, DC: The Cato Institute, 1987); Judith A. Baer, "The Fruitless Search for Original Intent," in *Judging the Constitution*, eds. Michael W. McCann and Gerald Houseman (Glenview, IL: Scott, Foresman and Co., 1989), pp. 49–71; Christopher E. Smith, "Jurisprudential Politics and the Manipulation of History," *The Western Journal of Black Studies*, 13 (1989): 156–61.

17. Justice Scalia, the Supreme Court's foremost proponent of orginalism, concedes that he would not follow that approach for Eighth Amendment cases concerning cruel and unusual punishments. Antonin Scalia, "Originalism: The Lesser Evil," *Cincinnati Law Review*, 57 (1989): 866.

18. *Baker v. Carr*, 369 U.S. 186, 267 (1962) (Frankfurter, J., Dissenting).

19. Herman Schwartz, *Packing the Courts: The Conservative Campaign to Rewrite the Constitution* (New York: Charles Scribner's Sons, 1988), pp. 3–9.

20. See Christopher E. Smith, "Bright-Line Rules and the Supreme Court: The Tension Between Clarity in Legal Doctrine and Justices' Policy Preferences," *Ohio Northern University Law Review*, 16 (1989), 119–37; Christopher E. Smith, "The Supreme Court's Emerging Majority: Restraining the High Court or Transforming Its Role?," *Akron Law Review*, 24 (1990): 393–421.

21. Louis Fisher, *American Constitutional Law* (New York: McGraw-Hill, 1990), p. 1319.

22. Ibid. pp. 1316–1317.

23. *Pollock v. Farmers' Loan and Trust Co.*, 157 U.S. 429 (1895).

24. *Oregon v. Mitchell*, 400 U.S. 112 (1970).

25. Ex parte McCardle, 74 U.S. 506 (1869).

26. *Watkins v. United States*, 354 U.S. 178 (1956).

27. *Barenblatt v. United States*, 360 U.S. 109 (1959).

28. Stephen Wasby, *The Supreme Court in the Federal Judicial System*, 3rd ed. (Chicago: Nelson-Hall, 1988), p. 309.

29. Fisher, *American Constitutional Law*, pp. 1321–1324.

30. Richard Kluger, *Simple Justice* (New York: Random House, 1975), pp. 613–14, 679, 695–99.

31. *Brown v. Board of Education*, 347 U.S. 483 (1954).

32. *Brown v. Board of Education*, 349 U.S. 294, 301 (1955).

33. See Joseph Burke, "The Cherokee Cases: A Study in Law, Politics, and Morality," *Stanford Law Review*, 21 (1971): 500–47.

34. Edwin Miles, "After John Marshall's Decision: *Worcester v. Georgia* and the Nullification Crisis," *Journal of Southern History*, 39 (1973): 519.

35. Lincoln Caplan, *The Tenth Justice* (New York: Random House, 1987), pp. 26–32.

36. Kluger, *Simple Justice*, pp. 665, 774.

Chapter 3: The Capacity of Courts as Policy-Making Forums

1. Donald Horowitz, *The Courts and Social Policy* (Washington, DC: Brookings Institution, 1977), p. 18.

2. Lawrence Baum, *The Supreme Court*, 3rd ed. (Washington, DC: Congressional Quarterly Press, 1989), p. 136.

3. See Christopher E. Smith, "Polarization and Change in the Federal Courts: *En Banc* Decisions in the U.S. Court of Appeals," *Judicature*, 74 (1900): 133–37.

4. Jeremy Rabkin, *Judicial Compulsion: How Public Law Distorts Public Policy* (New York: Basic Books, 1989), p. xiii.

5. See Abram Chayes, "The Role of the Judge in Public Law Litigation," *Harvard Law Review*, 89 (1976): 1281–1316.

6. See Horowitz, *The Courts and Social Policy*, pp. 22–67, 255–98.

7. Ralph K. Winter, Jr., "The Growth of Judicial Power," in *The Judiciary in a Democratic Society*, ed. Leonard J. Theberge (Lexington, MA: Lexington Books, 1979), p. 60.

8. Donald Horowitz, "The Courts as the Guardians of the Public Interest," *Public Administration Review*, 37 (1977): 152.

9. *Bowers v. Hardwick*, 478 U.S. 186 (1986).

10. Ibid., concerning opinion of Justice Lewis Powell.

11. See Richard Morgan, *Disabling America: The "Rights Industry" in Our Time* (New York: Basic Books, 1984), pp. 3–11, 74–133.

12. Rabkin, *Judicial Compulsions*, p. 20.

13. Richard Wilson, "Constraints of Power: The Constitutional Opinions of Judges Scalia, Bork, Posner, Easterbrook, and Winter," *University of Miami Law Review*, 40 (1986): 1181.

14. *DeFunis v. Odegaard*, 416 U.S. 312 (1974).

15. Marvin Frankel, "Partisan Justice," in *Readings on Adversarial Justice: The American Approach to Adjudication*, ed. Stephan Landsman (St. Paul, MN: West Publishing, 1988), p. 55.

16. See John H. Langbein, "The German Advantage in Civil Procedure," *University of Chicago Law Review*, 52 (1985): 823–66.

17. Nathan Glazer, "Should Judges Administer Social Services?," *The Public Interest*, 50 (1978): 79.

18. Stephen Wasby, "The Arrogation of Power or Accountability: 'Judicial Imperialism' Revisited," *Judicature*, 65 (1981): 215.

19. John W. Kingdon, *Agendas, Alternatives, and Public Policies* (Boston: Little, Brown and Co., 1984), pp. 99–100.

20. Wasby, "Arrogation of Power," p. 215.

21. Ibid.

22. Ibid., p. 216.

23. See Robert H. Mnookin and Lewis Kornhauser, "Bargaining in the Shadow of the Law: The Case of Divorce," *Yale Law Journal*, 88 (1979): 950–97.

24. See Colin S. Diver, "The Judge as Political Powerbroker: Superintending Structural Change in Public Institutions," *Virginia Law Review*, 65 (1979): 43–106.

25. Judith Resnik, "Managerial Judges," *Harvard Law Review*, 96 (1982): 377.

26. See *Newman v. Alabama*, 349 F.Supp. 278 (M.D. Ala. 1972); *Pugh v. Locke*, 406 F.Supp. 318 (M.D. Ala. 1976).

27. Tinsley E. Yarbrough, "The Alabama Prison Litigation," *The Justice System Journal*, 9 (1984): 276–90.

28. Phillip J. Cooper, *Hard Judicial Choices* (New York: Oxford University Press, 1988), pp. 337–38.

29. See Geoffrey P. Alpert, Ben M. Crouch, and C. Ronald Huff, "Prison Reform by Judicial Decree: The Unintended Consequences of *Ruiz v. Estelle*," *The Justice System Journal*, 9 (1984): 291–305.

30. See Lino A. Graglia, *Disaster By Decree* (Ithaca, NY: Cornell University Press, 1976), pp. 203–83.

31. See Gary Orfield, *Must We Bus?: Segregated Schools and National Policy* (Washington, DC: Brookings Institution, 1978), pp. 62–67, 119–26; Meyer Weinberg, "The Relationship Between School Desegregation and Academic Achievement: A Review of the Research," in *The Courts, Social Science, and School Desegregation*, eds. Betsy Levin and Willis D. Hawley (New Brunswick, NJ: Transaction Books, 1977), pp. 241–70; Thomas F. Pettigrew, "A Sociological View of the Post-*Bradley* Era," *Wayne Law Review*, 21 (1975): 813–32.

32. *Milliken v. Bradley*, 418 U.S. 717 (1974).

33. Richard Kluger, *Simple Justice: The History of Brown v. Board of Education and Black America's Struggle for Equality* (New York: Random House, 1975), pp. 771–73.

34. Rober Pear, "Social Security Stalls Disabled Children Aid," *Akron Beacon Journal*, Nov. 20, 1990. p. A1.

35. Ibid.

36. See Charles A. Johnson and Bradley C. Canon, *Judicial Policies: Implementation and Impact* (Washington, DC: Congressional Quarterly Press, 1984).

37. *Miranda v. Arizona*, 384 U.S. 436 (1966).

38. *Engel v. Vitale*, 370 U.S. 421 (1962).

39. Traciel V. Reid, "Judicial Policy-Making and Implementation: An Empirical Examination," *Western Political Quarterly*, 41 (1988): 509–27.

40. Stephen Wasby, "The Communication of Supreme Court's Criminal Procedure Decisions: A Preliminary Mapping," *Villanova Law Review*, 18 (1973): 1086–1118.

41. Neal Milner, "Comparative Analysis of Patterns of Compliance with Supreme Court Decisions," *Law and Society Review*, 5 (1970): 119–34.

42. Ibid, p. 123.

43. Kenneth M. Dolbeare and Phillip E. Hammond, "Inertia in Midway: Supreme Court Decisions and Local Responses," *Journal of Legal Education*, 23 (1970): 112.

44. Ibid., pp. 115–16.

45. See Charles S. Bullock, III and Charles M. Lamb, "Toward a Theory of Civil Rights Implementation," *American Court Systems*, 2nd ed., eds. Sheldon Goldman and Austin Sarat (New York: Longman, 1989), pp. 559–68.

Chapter 4: School Desegregation: Federal Judicial Power and Social Change

1. See Eugene Genovese, *Roll, Jordon, Roll: The World the Slaves Made* (New York: Random House, 1972), p. 31; Lerone Bennett, *Before the Mayflower*, 5th ed. (New York: Penguin, 1982), pp. 44–45.

2. See Gunnar Myrdal, *An American Dilemma: The Negro Problem and Modern Democracy* (New York: Harper and Row, 1944).

3. See *Civil Rights Cases*, 109 U.S. 3 (1883).

4. See *Plessy v. Ferguson*, 163 U.S. 537 (1896).

5. Stuart Taylor, Jr., "Meese v. Brennan: Who's Right About the Constitution," *The New Republic*, Jan. 6, 13, 1986, p. 21.

6. Stephen Wasby, "The NAACP and the LDF," *Judicature*, 68 (1985): 342–43.

7. Richard Kluger, *Simple Justice: The History of* Brown v. Board of Education *and Black America's Struggle for Equality* (New York: Random House, 1975), pp. 125–213.

8. *Plessy v. Ferguson*, 163 U.S. 537 (1896).

9. *Pearson v. Murray*, 182 A. 593 (Md. 1936).

10. *Missouri* ex rel. *Gaines v. Canada*, 305 U.S. 337 (1938).

11. *Sipuel v. Board of Regents*, 332 U.S. 631 (1948).

12. *Sweatt v. Painter*, 339 U.S. 629 (1950).

13. *McLaurin v. Oklahoma Board of Regents*, 339 U.S. 637 (1950).

14. Kluger, *Simple Justice*, p. 187.

15. Donald G. Nieman, *Promises to Keep: African-Americans and the Constitutional Order, 1776 to the Present* (New York: Oxford University Press, 1991), p. 168.

16. *Brown v. Board of Education*, 347 U.S. 483 (1954).

17. Stephen L. Wasby, "Civil Rights Litigation by Organizations: Constraints and Choices," *Judicature*, 68 (1985): 346.

18. Derrick A. Bell, Jr., "Serving Two Masters: Integration Ideals and Client Interests in School Desegregation Litigation," in *Limits of Justice: The Courts' Role in School Desegregation*, eds. Howard I. Kalodner and James J. Fishman (Cambridge, MA: Ballinger Publishing, 1978), pp. 583–87.

19. Kluger, *Simple Justice*, pp. 678–83.

20. Ibid., p. 698.

21. Lincoln Caplan, *The Tenth Justice: The Solicitor General and the Rule of the Law* (New York: Random House, 1987), p. 26.

22. *Brown v. Board of Education*, 349 U.S. 294, 301 (1955).

23. Caplan, *The Tenth Justice*, pp. 26–27.

24. Barbara Flicker, "The View From the Bench: Judges in Desegregation Cases," in *Justice and School Systems: The Role of the Courts in Education Litigation*, ed. Barbara Flicker (Philadelphia, PA: Temple University Press, 1990), p. 365.

25. See Harry P. Stumpf, *American Judicial Politics* (New York: Harcourt Brace Jovanovich, 1988), pp. 189–210.

26. Richard E. Morgan, *Disabling America: The 'Rights Industry' in Our Time* (New York: Basic Books, 1984), p. 62.

27. Bernard Schwartz, *Swann's Way: The School Busing Case and The Supreme Court* (New York: Oxford University Press, 1986), p. 4.

28. Marian Wright Edelman, "Southern School Desegregation, 1954–1973: A Judicial-Political Overview," *The Annals of the American Academy of Political and Social Science*, 407 (1973): 37–38.

29. Schwartz, *Swann's Way*, p. 8.

30. *Alexander v. Holmes County Board of Education*, 396 S. Ct. 19, 20 (1969).

31. *Swann v. Charlotte-Mecklenburg Board of Education*, 401 U.S. 1 (1971).

32. See Lino Graglia, *Disaster By Decree: The Supreme Court Decisions on Race and the Schools* (Ithaca, NY: Cornell University Press, 1976).

33. Gary Orfield, *Must We Bus?: Segregated Schools and National Policy* (Washington, DC: Brookings Institution, 1978), p. 253.

34. See Christopher E. Smith, " 'What If. . . .': Critical Junctures on the Road to (In)Equality," *Thurgood Marshall Law Review*, 15 (1989–90): 10–17.

35. See Orfield, *Must We Bus?*, pp. 30–36.

36. *Milliken v. Bradley*, 418 U.S. 717 (1974).

37. Alfred H. Kelly, Winfred A. Harbison, and Herman Belz, *The American Constitution: Its Origins and Development*, Vol. II, 7th ed. (New York: W. W. Norton, 1991), pp. 684–85.

38. Nieman, *Promises to Keep*, p. 200.

39. Graglia, *Disaster by Decree*, p. 279.

40. See Christine H. Rossell, "Desegregation Plans, Racial Isolation, White Flight, and Community Response," in *The Consequences of School Desegregation*. eds. Christine H. Rossell and Willis D. Hawley (Philadelphia, PA: Temple University Press, 1983), pp. 13–39.

41. Rita E. Mahard and Robert L. Crain, "Research on Minority Achievement in Desegregated Schools," in *The Consequences of School Desegregation*. eds. Christine H. Rossell and Willis D. Hawley (Philadelphia, PA: Temple University Press, 1983), pp. 103–25.

42. Orfield, *Must We Bus?*, pp. 123–24.

43. Janet Ward Schofield and H. Andrew Sagar, "Desegregation, School Practices, and Student Race Relations," in *The Consequences of School Desegregation*. eds. Christine H. Rossell and Willis D. Hawley (Philadelphia, PA: Temple University Press), pp. 67–68.

44. Orfield, *Must We Bus?*, p. 133.

45. Ibid., pp. 391–420.

46. See "A Tale of Four Cities," *Time*, Sept. 17, 1979, pp. 76–78; Chester E. Finn, Jr., "Choice and Coercion," *The New Republic*, Mar. 11, 1985, pp. 35–39.

47. See "A Tale of Four Cities," p. 76; Flicker, "The View From the Bench," p. 375.

48. Rossell, "Desegregation Plans, Racial Isolation," p. 50.

49. Schwartz, *Swann's Way*, p. 21.

50. Ibid., pp. 190–92.

51. Ibid., p. 191.

52. Orfield, *Must We Bus?*, p. 18.

53. Christopher E. Smith, "The Supreme Court and Ethnicity," *Oregon Law Review*, 69 (1990): 805–12.

54. Robert Dahl, *Democracy in the United States*, 4th ed. (Boston: Houghton Mifflin, 1981), p. 162.

55. Laurence H. Tribe, "The Curvature of Constitutional Space: What Lawyers Can Learn From Modern Physics," *Harvard Law Review*, 103 (1989): 29.

56. Lawrence Baum, *The Supreme Court*, 3rd. ed. (Washington, DC: Congressional Quarterly Press, 1989), p. 242.

57. Ibid.

58. Stuart Scheingold, "Constitutional Rights and Social Change: Civil Rights in Perspective," in *Judging the Constitution: Critical Essays on Judicial Lawmaking*. eds. Michael McCann and Gerald Houseman (Glenview, IL: Scott, Foresman, 1989), p. 80.

59. Ibid.

60. Michael Parenti, *Democracy for the Few*, 5th ed. (New York: St. Martin's Press, 1988), p. 293.

61. See Gerald Rosenberg, *The Hollow Hope: Can Courts Bring About Social Change?* (Chicago: University of Chicago Press, 1991).

62. Tribe, "The Curvature of Constitutional Space," p. 30.

Chapter 5: Education Financing: Judicial Policy-Making in State Courts

1. Stephen L. Wasby, *The Supreme Court in the Federal Judicial System*, 3rd ed. (Chicago: Nelson-Hall, 1988), p. 2.

2. *Martin v. Hunter's Lessee*, 14 U.S. (1 Wheat.) 304 (1816); *Cohens v. Virginia*, 19 U.S. (6 Wheat.) 264 (1821).

3. See Stanley H. Friedelbaum, "Independent State Grounds: Contemporary Invitations to Judicial Activism," in *State Supreme Courts: Policymakers in the Federal System*, eds. Mary Cornelia Porter and G. Alan Tarr (Westport, CT: Greenwood Press, 1982), pp. 23–53.

4. See G. Edward White, *Tort Law in America: An Intellectual History* (New York: Oxford University Press, 1985), pp. 114–38, 180–210.

5. Robert A. Dahl, *Democracy in the United States: Promise and Performance*, 4th ed. (Boston: Houghton Mifflin, 1981), p. 443.

6. James S. Coleman, "The Concept of Equality in Educational Opportunity," in *Equal Education Opportunity* (Cambridge, MA: Harvard University, 1968), p. 14.

7. Quoted in Alan B. Wilson, "Social Class and Equal Opportunity," in *Equal Educational Opportunity* (Cambridge, MA: Harvard University Press, 1968), p. 81.

8. "School Finances: Rich Districts, Poor Districts," *Akron Beacon Journal*, March 18, 1990, p. F2.

9. David B. Tyack, *The One Best System: A History of American Urban Education* (Cambridge, MA: Harvard University Press, 1974), p. 272.

10. Ibid., p. 273.

11. Ibid., pp. 275–84.

12. Peter Irons, *The Courage of Their Convictions: Sixteen Americans Who Fought Their Way to the Supreme Court* (New York: Penguin, 1990), p. 287.

13. Ibid.

14. Ibid., pp. 285–88.

15. See James L. Gibson, "From Simplicity to Complexity: The Development of Theory in the Study of Judicial Behavior," *Political Behavior*, 5 (1983): 7–49.

16. See Christopher E. Smith, "Polarization and Change in the Federal Courts: *En Banc* Decisions in the U.S. Courts of Appeals," *Judicature*, 74 (1990): 133–37.

17. See C. Neal Tate and Roger Handberg, "Time Binding and Theory Building in Personal Attribute Models of Supreme Court Voting Behavior, 1916–1988," *American Journal of Political Science*, 35 (1991): 460–80.

18. *San Antonio Independent School District v. Rodriguez*, 93 S. Ct. 1278 (1973).

19. *San Antonio Independent School District v. Rodriguez*, 93 S. Ct. 1278, 1316 (Marshall, J., dissenting).

20. Christopher E. Smith, *Courts and the Poor* (Chicago: Nelson-Hall, 1991), pp. 73–119.

21. Gayle Binion, "The Disadvantaged Before the Burger Court," *Law and Policy Quarterly*, 4 (1982): 58.

22. Robert W. Bennett, "The Burger Court and the Poor," in *The Burger Court: The Counter-Revolution That Wasn't*, ed. Vincent Blasi (New Haven, CT: Yale University Press, 1983), p. 55.

23. Archibald Cox, *The Court and the Constitution* (Boston: Houghton Mifflin, 1987), p. 313.

24. Ibid.

25. Richard E. Morgan, *Disabling America: The "Rights Industry" in Our Time* (New York: Basic Books, 1984), p. 204.

26. *Missouri v. Jenkins*, 110 S. Ct. 1651 (1990). See also Greenhouse, "Courts Says Judge May Order Taxes to Alleviate Bias," *New York Times*, April 19, 1990, p. A1.

27. See William J. Brennan, "State Constitutions and the Protection of Individual Rights," *Harvard Law Review*, 90 (1977): 489–504.

28. David W. Neubauer, *Judicial Process: Law, Courts, and Politics in the United States* (Pacific Grove, CA: Brooks/Cole, 1991), p. 354.

29. See Christopher E. Smith, *Courts, Politics, and the Judicial Process* (Chicago: Nelson-Hall, 1993), chapter 4.

30. *Serrano v. Priest*, 487 P.2d 1241 (Cal. 1971).

31. William E. Thro, "The Third Wave: The Impact of the Montana, Kentucky, and Texas Decisions on the Future of Public School Finance Reform Litigation," *Journal of Law and Education*, 19 (1990): 223–25.

32. *Robinson v. Cahill*, 303 A.2d 273 (N.J. 1973).

33. Thro, "The Third Wave," p. 228.

34. Ibid., p. 229–32.

35. Woody Barwick, "A Chronology of the Kentucky Case," *Journal of Education Finance*, 15 (1989): 136–41.

36. Thro, "The Third Wave," p. 235.

37. Howard LaFranchi, "School Tax Inequities Vex Texas," *Christian Science Monitor*, Sept. 9, 1988, p. 17.

38. *Edgewood Independent School District v. Kirby* (1989) discussed in Susan Tifft, "The Big Shift in School Finance," *Time*, Oct. 16, 1989, p. 48.

39. "Texas Judge Supports New Law on Financing for Poorer Schools," *New York Times*, April 16, 1991, p. A12.

40. William E. Camp and David C. Thompson, "School Finance Litigation: Legal Issues and Politics of Reform," *Journal of Education Finance*, 14 (1988): 223.

41. Donald W. Crowley, "Implementing *Serrano*: A Study of Judicial Impact," *Law and Policy Quarterly*, 4 (1982): 304.

42. Ibid.

43. Annette B. Johnson, "State Court Intervention in School Finance Reform," *Cleveland State Law Review*, 28 (1979): 349–50.

44. Crowley, "Implementing Serrano," p. 319.

45. Richard A. L. Gambitta, "Litigation, Judicial Deference, and Policy Change," *Law and Policy Quarterly*, 3 (1981): 158.

46. Billy D. Walker and John D. Thompson, "Special Report: The Texas Supreme Court and Edgewood I.S.D. v. Kirby," *Journal of Education Finance*, 15 (1990): 416.

47. Camp and Thompson, "School Finance Litigation," pp. 224–31.

48. "Texas Judge Supports New Law," p. A12.

49. Johnson, "State Court Intervention," pp. 344–45 n. 80.

50. Camp and Thompson, "School Finance Litigation," p. 223.

51. Lonnie Harp, "After First Year, Ky. Reforms Called 'On the Move'," *Education Week*, 10 (Apr. 19, 1991): 1, 20, 22.

52. Ibid., p. 20.

53. Gerald M. Stern, *The Buffalo Creek Disaster* (New York: Random House, 1976), pp. 52–57.

54. See Sam Howe Verhovek, "Poorer New York School Districts Challenging State Aid as Unequal," *New York Times*, May 6, 1991, p. A1.

Chapter 6: Prison Reform Litigation: Judicial Power and Institutional Administration

1. See *Ruffin v. Commonwealth*, 62 Va. 790, 796 (1871).

2. See *Banning v. Looney*, 213 F.2d 771 (10th Cir. 1954).

3. *Cooper v. Pate*, 378 U.S. 546 (1964).

4. See Christopher E. Smith and J. Marc Valencia, "Black Muslims and the Development of Prisoners' Rights," *Journal of Black Studies*, (forthcoming 1993).

5. See *Holt v. Sarver*, 309 F.Supp. 362 (E.D. Ark. 1970); *Hutto v. Finney*, 437 U.S. 678 (1978).

6. Larry W. Yackle, *Reform and Regret: The Story of Federal Judicial Involvement in the Alabama Prison System* (New York: Oxford University Press, 1989), p. 256.

7. See Stuart Scheingold, *The Politics of Law and Order* (New York: Longman, 1984), pp. 37–57.

8. Jim Thomas, Devin Keeler, and Kathy Harris, "Issues and Misconceptions in Prisoner Litigation: A Critical View," *Criminology*, 24 (1986): 790.

9. "Prisoners in 1989," *Bureau of Justice Statistics Bulletin*, May 1990, p. 1.

10. See Christopher E. Smith, "Examining the Boundaries of *Bounds:* Prison Law Libraries and Access to the Courts," *Howard Law Journal*, 30 (1987): 27–44.

11. See Donald H. Zeigler and Michele G. Hermann, "The Invisible Litigant: An Inside View of Pro Se Actions in the Federal Courts," *New York University Law Review*, 47 (1972): 157–257.

12. Roger A. Hanson, "What Should Be Done When Prisoners Want to Take the State to Court?," *Judicature*, 70 (1987): 225.

13. See William Bennett Turner, "When Prisoners Sue: A Study of Prisoner Section 1983 Suits in the Federal Courts," *Harvard Law Review*, (1979): 610–63.

14. Hanson, "What Should Be Done," p. 225.

15. Christopher E. Smith, *United States Magistrates in the Federal Courts: Subordinate Judges* (New York: Praeger Publishers, 1990), pp. 176–77.

16. John J. DiIulio, Jr., "The Old Regime and the *Ruiz* Revolution: The Impact of Judicial Intervention on Texas Prisons," in *Courts, Corrections, and the Constitution*, ed. John J. DiIulio, Jr. (New York: Oxford University Press, 1990), p. 59.

17. Bradley S. Chilton and Susette Talarico, "Politics and Constitutional Interpretation in Prison Reform Litigation: The Case of *Guthrie v. Evans*," in *Courts, Corrections, and the Constitution*, ed. John DiIulio, Jr. (New York: Oxford University Press, 1990), p. 124.

18. DiIulio, "The Old Regime," p. 59.

19. Chilton and Talarico, "Politics and Constitutional Interpretation," p. 118.

20. See Clair A. Cripe, "Courts, Corrections, and the Constitution: A Practitioner's View," in *Courts, Corrections, and the Constitution*, ed. John DiIulio, Jr. (New York: Oxford University Press, 1990), pp. 268–86.

21. Christopher E. Smith, "United States Magistrates and the Processing of Prisoner Litigation," *Federal Probation*, 52 (Dec. 1988): 17.

22. Phillip J. Cooper, *Hard Judicial Choices* (New York: Oxford University Press, 1988), p. 255.

23. Tinsley E. Yarbrough, "The Alabama Prison Litigation," *The Justice System Journal*, 9 (1984): 278–79.

24. Ibid., p. 280.

25. Chilton and Talarico, "Politics and Constitutional Interpretation," p. 119.

26. Cripe, "Courts, Corrections, and the Constitution," p. 274.

27. Chilton and Talarico, "Politics and Constitutional Interpretation," p. 124.

28. Ibid.

29. See *Rhodes v. Chapman*, 452 U.S. 337 (1981).

30. Malcolm M. Feeley and Roger A. Hanson, "The Impact of Judicial Intervention on Prisons and Jails: A Framework for Analysis and a Review of the Literature," in *Courts, Corrections, and the Constitution*, ed. John J. DiIulio, Jr. (New York: Oxford University Press, 1990), p. 29.

31. Ibid., p. 27.

32. Robert C. Bradley, "Judicial Appointment and Judicial Intervention: The Issuance of Structural Reform Decrees in Correctional Litigation," in *Courts, Corrections, and the Constitution*, ed. John J. DiIulio, Jr. (New York: Oxford University Press, 1990), pp. 249–67.

33. M. Kay Harris and Dudley P. Spiller, Jr., *After Decision: Implementation of Judicial Decrees in Correctional Settings* (Washington, DC: Law Enforcement Assistance Administration, 1977), p. 11.

34. John J. DiIulio, Jr., "Conclusion: What Judges Can Do to Improve Prisons and Jails," in *Courts, Corrections, and the Constitution*, ed. John J. DiIulio, Jr. (New York: Oxford University Press, 1990), pp. 287–91.

35. Cripe, "Courts, Corrections, and the Constitution," pp. 275–84.

36. Feeley and Hanson, "The Impact of Judicial Intervention," p. 27.

37. James B. Jacobs, *Stateville: The Penitentiary in Mass Society* (Chicago: University of Chicago Press, 1977), p. 204.

38. See Geoffrey P. Alpert, Ben M. Crouch, and C. Ronald Huff, "Prison Reform by Judicial Decree: The Unintended Consequences of *Ruiz v. Estelle*," *The Justice System Journal*, 9 (1984): 291–305.

39. Sheldon Ekland-Olson, "Crowding, Social Control, and Prison Violence: Evidence from the Post-*Ruiz* Years in Texas," *Law and Society Review*, 20 (1986): 404.

40. Feeley and Hanson, "The Impact of Judicial Intervention," pp. 18–21.

41. Linda Harriman and Jeffrey D. Straussman, "Do Judges Determine Budget Decisions? Federal Court Decisions in Prison Reform and State Spending for Corrections," *Public Administration Review*, 43 (1983): 350.

42. William A. Taggart, "Refining the Power of the Federal Judiciary: The Impact of Court-Ordered Prison Reform on State Expenditures for Corrections," *Law and Society Review*, 23 (1989): 241–71.

43. Malcolm M. Feeley, "The Significance of Prison Conditions: Budgets and Regions," *Law and Society Review*, 23 (1989): 281.

44. See George E. Hale, "Federal Courts and the State Budgetary Process," *Administration and Society*, 11 (1979): 357–68.

45. Cripe, "Courts, Corrections, and the Constitution," p. 283.

46. Administrative Office of the U.S. Courts, *Annual Reprint of the Director of the Administrative Office at the U.S. Courts* (1990), p. 138.

47. Thomas, Keeler, and Harris, "Issues and Misconceptions," p. 790.

48. George F. Cole and Jonathan E. Silbert, "Alternative Dispute-Resolution Mechanisms for Prisoner Grievances," *The Justice System Journal*, 9 (1984): 306–24.

49. Feeley and Hanson, "The Impact of Judicial Intervention," pp. 31–32.

50. See Christopher E. Smith, "Federal Judges' Role in Prisoner Litigation: What's Necessary? What's Proper?," *Judicature*, 70 (1986): 144–50.

51. See DiIulio, "What Judges Can Do," pp. 287–320.

52. See *Bell v. Wolfish*, 441 U.S. 520 (1979); *Rhodes v. Chapman*, 452 U.S. 337 (1981); *Wilson v. Seiter*, 111 S. Ct. 2321 (1991).

53. Bureau of Justice Statistics, "Prisoners in 1989," p. 1.

Chapter 7: Abortion: The Judiciary's Interactions with Other Political Actors

1. *Dred Scott v. Sandford*, 60 U.S. (19 How.) 393 (1857).

2. Archibald Cox, *The Court and the Constitution* (Boston: Houghton Mifflin, 1987), p. 322.

3. *Roe v. Wade*, 410 U.S. 113 (1973).

4. See Patricia G. Steinhoff and Milton Diamond, *Abortion Politics: The Hawaii Experience* (Honolulu: University Press of Hawaii, 1977).

5. Raymond Tatalovich and Byron W. Daynes, *The Politics of Abortion: A Study in Community Conflict in Public Policymaking* (New York: Praeger Publishers, 1981), p. 154.

6. Ibid., p. 164.

7. David O'Brien, *Storm Center: The Supreme Court in American Politics,* 2nd ed. (New York: W. W. Norton, 1990), p. 40.

8. Alain L. Sanders, "The Marble Palace's Southern Gentleman," *Time,* July 9, 1990, p. 13.

9. Ibid.

10. *Webster v. Reproductive Health Services,* 109 S. Ct. 3040, 3065-3066 (1989) (Scalia J., dissenting).

11. "Scalia Steers Non-Controversial Path During Lecture at Cleveland College," *Akron Beacon Journal,* Oct. 25, 1989, p. C2.

12. Raymond Tatalovich, "Abortion: Prochoice Versus Prolife," in *Social Regulatory Policy: Moral Controversies in American Politics,* eds. Raymond Tatalovich and Byron W. Daynes (Boulder, CO: Westview Press, 1988), pp. 186–89.

13. O'Brien, *Storm Center,* p. 41.

14. Ibid., p. 41.

15. Louis Fisher, *American Constitutional Law* (New York: McGraw-Hill, 1990), p. 1150.

16. Stephen L. Wasby, *The Supreme Court in the Federal Judicial System,* 3rd ed. (Chicago: Nelson-Hall, 1988), pp. 308–309.

17. Sheldon Goldman and Thomas Jahnige, *The Federal Courts as a Political System,* 3rd ed. (New York: Harper and Row, 1985), pp. 5–6, 206–33.

18. *Harris v. McRae,* 448 U.S. 297 (1980).

19. *Williams v. Zbaraz,* 448 U.S. 358 (1980).

20. Fisher, *American Constitutional Law,* p. 1150.

21. *City of Akron v. Akron Center for Reproductive Health,* 103 S. Ct. 2481, 2489 n. 5 (1983).

22. *Roe v. Wade,* 410 U.S. 113, 159 (1973).

23. See *Thornburgh v. American College of Obstetricians and Gynecologists,* 476 U.S. 747 (1986).

24. See Lincoln Caplan, *The Tenth Justice: The Solicitor General and the Rule of Law* (New York: Random House, 1987), pp. 135–54.

25. Herman Schwartz, *Packing the Courts: The Conservative Campaign to Rewrite the Constitution* (New York: Charles Scribner's Sons, 1988), pp. 58–62, 94–95.

26. See James L. Gibson, "From Simplicity to Complexity: The Development of Theory in the Study of Judicial Behavior," *Political Behavior,* 5 (1983): 7–49.

27. Steve Alumbaugh and C.K. Rowland, "The Links Between Platform-Based Appointment Criteria and Trial Judges' Abortion Judgments," *Judicature,* 74 (1990): 162.

28. Aaron Epstein, "Reagan Leaving Mighty Legal Legacy," *Akron Beacon Journal*, Nov. 24, 1988, p. G5.

29. Neil A. Lewis, "Bush Travels Reagan's Course in Naming Judges," *New York Times*, Apr. 10, 1990, p. A1.

30. See Christopher E. Smith, "Polarization and Change in the Federal Courts: *En Banc* Decisions in the U.S. Courts of Appeals," *Judicature*, 74 (1990): 133–37.

31. "No Heavy Lifting at the High Court," *Newsweek*, Feb. 5, 1990, p. 63.

32. O'Brien, *Storm Center*, p. 103.

33. *City of Akron v. Akron Center for Reproductive Health*, 103 S. Ct. 2481, 2504–2516 (O'Connor, J., dissenting).

34. See Laurence Tribe, *God Save This Honorable Court: How the Choice of Supreme Court Justices Shapes Our History* (New York: New American Library, 1985), pp. 117–21.

35. See Maureen Dowd, "Souter, New Hampshire Judge Named by Bush for High Court; No 'Litmus Test,' President Says: Abortion Minimized," *New York Times*, July 24, 1990, p. A1.

36. Schwartz, *Packing the Courts*, pp. 125–43.

37. *Webster v. Reproductive Health Services*, 109 S. Ct. 3040 (1989).

38. Ibid.

39. *Ohio v. Akron Center for Reproductive Health*, 110 S. Ct. 2972 (1990). See also Greenhouse, "States May Require Girl to Notify Parents Before Having Abortion," *New York Times*, June 26, 1990, p. A1.

40. *Rust v. Sullivan* (1991), discussed in Greenhouse, "5 Justices Uphold U.S. Rule Curbing Abortion Advice," *New York Times*, May 24, 1991, p. A1.

41. *Planned Parenthood v. Casey*, 112 S. Ct. 2791 (1992).

42. "Countdown: The Wars Within the States," *Newsweek*, July 17, 1989, p. 24.

43. Christopher E. Smith, *Courts and the Poor* (Chicago: Nelson-Hall, 1991), pp. 117–18.

44. "Abortion Bill Veto is Upheld in North Dakota," *New York Times*, Apr. 3, 1991, p. A13.

45. "Abortion Rights Law Upheld in Recount," *Akron Beacon Journal*, Dec. 15, 1991, p. A4.

46. *Committee to Defend Reproductive Rights v. Myers*, 625 P.2d 779 (Cal. 1981).

47. Judy Daubenmier, "Ban on Abortion Aid Killed," *Akron Beacon Journal*, Feb. 21, 1991, p. A7.

48. Paul Anderson and Mark Silva, "Florida Abortion Right Upheld," *Miami Herald*, Oct. 6, 1989, p. A1.

Chapter 8: Tort Law: The Cumulative Policy Consequences of Litigation

1. James S. Kakalik and Nicholas M. Pace, *Costs and Compensation Paid in Tort Litigation* (Santa Monica, CA: The RAND Corp., 1986), pp. vi–x.

2. American International Group (AIG), "Why Reforming Our Liability System is Essential If American Is to Succeed in Overseas Markets," *Time,* Apr. 8, 1991, p. 78.

3. Kenneth S. Abraham, "The Causes of the Insurance Crisis," in *New Directions in Liability Law,* Walter Olson ed. (New York: Academy of Political Science, 1988), p. 64.

4. Ibid.

5. "Man Who Lost Eye With Drug Awarded $127 Million By Jury," *Akron Beacon Journal,* Oct. 20, 1991, p. A3.

6. Peter W. Huber, *Liability: The Legal Revolution and Its Consequences* (New York: Basic Books, 1988), p. 159.

7. Edith Stokey and Richard Zeckhauser, *A Primer for Policy Analysis* (New York: W. W. Norton, 1978), p. 3.

8. Peter Huber, "Knowledge of the Law Is No Excuse," in *New Directions in Tort Liability,* Walter Olson ed. (New York: Academy of Political Science, 1988), p. 158.

9. Edward Levi, *An Introduction to Legal Reasoning* (Chicago: University of Chicago Press, 1948), pp. 1–7.

10. Walter F. Murphy and C. Herman Pritchett, *Courts, Politics, and Judges: An Introduction to the Judicial Process,* 4th ed. (New York: Random House, 1986), pp. 389–90.

11. Kermit L. Hall, *The Magic Mirror: Law in American History* (New York: Oxford University Press, 1989), p. 297.

12. William L. Prosser, John W. Wade, and Victor E. Schwartz, *Torts: Cases and Materials,* 7th ed. (Mineola, NY: The Foundation Press, 1982), p. 143.

13. G. Edward White, *Tort Law in America: An Intellectual History* (New York: Oxford University Press, 1985), p. 16.

14. *Farwell v. Boston and Worcester Railroad Corp.,* 45 Mass. 49 (1942).

15. Hall, *Magic Mirror,* p. 125.

16. Ibid., p. 126.

17. Ibid., pp. 125–26.

18. *McPherson v. Buick Motor Co.,* 217 N.Y. 382 (1916), *discussed in* Huber, *Liability,* p. 35.

19. Huber, *Liability,* p. 38.

20. Ibid., p. 39.

21. Ibid., p. 40.

22. George L. Priest, "Understanding the Liability Crisis," in *New Directions in Liability Law,* Walter Olson ed. (New York: Academy of Political Science, 1988), p. 204.

23. Huber, *Liability,* p. 75–78.

24. Reid Hastie, Steven D. Penrod, and Nancy Pennington, *Inside the Jury* (Cambridge, MA: Harvard University Press, 1983), p. 137.

25. See Shari Seidman Diamond, "Scientific Jury Selection: What Social Scientists Know and Do Not Know," *Judicature,* 4 (1990): 178–83.

26. Valerie P. Hans and Neil Vidmar, *Judging the Jury* (New York: Plenum Press, 1986), pp. 79–80, 87–88.

27. Diamond, "Scientific Jury Selection," p. 183.

28. Ibid.

29. Huber, *Liability*, pp. 121–22.

30. M.E. Freeman-Parsons, "Woman, 96, Wins $1.5 Million in Suit Against Tabloid," *Akron Beacon Journal*, Dec. 6, 1991, p. A10.

31. Mark Peterson, Syam Sarma and Michael Shanley, *Punitive Damages: Empirical Findings* (Santa Monica, CA: The RAND Corp., 1987), pp. v–vi.

32. James P. Levine, *Juries and Politics* (Pacific Grove, CA: Brooks/Cole Publishing, 1992), p. 176.

33. See Jethro K. Lieberman, *The Litigious Society* (New York: Basic Books, 1981), pp. 85–87.

34. National Center for State Courts, *State Court Caseload Statistics: Annual Report 1988* (Williamsburg, VA: National Center for State Courts, 1990), pp. 54, 59–60.

35. Don Bandy, "$1.2 Million to Be Paid in Stray-Bullet Death," *Akron Beacon Journal*, Dec. 3, 1991, p. B6.

36. Lawrence M. Friedman, *Total Justice* (Boston: Beacon Press, 1985), p. 5.

37. See Lieberman, *The Litigious Society*, pp. 5–10.

38. See Barbara A. Curran, "American Lawyers in the 1980s: A Profession in Transition," *Law and Society Review*, 20 (1986): 19–51.

39. Lance Morrow, "A Nation of Finger Pointers," *Time*, Aug. 12, 1991, p. 15.

40. "Confessed Mass-Slayer Dahmer Sued for $3 Billion by Missing Man's Kin," *Akron Beacon Journal*, Dec. 5, 1991, p. A22.

41. Mark A. Peterson, *Compensation for Injuries: Civil Jury Verdicts in Cook County* (Santa Monica, CA: The RAND Corp., 1984), p. ix. See also Michael G. Shanley and Mark A. Peterson, *Comparative Justice: Civil Jury Verdicts in San Francisco and Cook Counties, 1959–1980* (Santa Monica, CA: The RAND Corp., 1983), p. xii.

42. Michael G. Shanley and Mark A. Peterson, *Posttrial Adjustments to Jury Awards* (Santa Monica, CA: The RAND Corp., 1987), p. viii.

43. Marc Galanter, "Reading the Landscape of Disputes: What We Know and Don't Know (and Think We Know) About Our Allegedly Contentious and Litigious Society," *U.C.L.A. Law Review*, 31 (1983): 51–61.

44. Remarks of Chief Justice Warren E. Burger at the Arthur T. Vanderbilt dinner, New York City, Nov. 18, 1982, quoted in Harry P. Stumpf, *American Judicial Politics* (New York: Harcout Brace Jovanovich, 1988), p. 295.

45. "People Hurt By Doctors Rarely Sue," *Akron Beacon Journal*, July 25, 1991, p. A13.

46. See Richard E. Miller and Austin Sarat, "Grievances, Claims, and Disputes: Assessing the Adversary Culture," *Law and Society Review*, 15 (1980–81): 525–65; William L. Felstiner, Richard L. Abel, and Austin Sarat, "The Emergence and Transformation of Disputes: Naming, Blaming, Claiming . . .," *Law and Society Review*, 15 (1980–81): 631–54.

47. Richard L. Abel, "The Crisis Is Injuries, Not Liability," in *New Directions in Tort Law*, Walter Olson ed. (New York: The Academy of Political Science, 1988), pp. 31–41.

48. Stumpf, *American Judicial Politics*, p. 296.

49. See Janice Castro, "Condition: Critical," *Time*, Nov. 25, 1991, p. 40.

50. Analysts have discounted industry collusion as the sole cause of the insurance crisis. See Abraham, "The Causes of the Insurance Crisis," pp. 54–66.

51. Andrea Sachs, "A Blow to Big Business," *Time*, Mar. 18, 1991, p. 71.

52. Ibid.

53. *Pacific Mutual Life Insurance Co. v. Haslip*, 111 S. Ct. 1032 (1991).

54. American International Group, pp. 78–79.

55. Philip J. Hilts, "Bush Seeks Awards Limit for Medical Malpractice," *Akron Beacon Journal*, May 13, 1991, p. A1.

56. See *Agenda for Civil Justice Reform in America: A Report from President's Council on Competitiveness* (August 1991), pp. 1–9.

57. Michael Duffy, "Need Friends in High Places?," *Time*, Nov. 4, 1991, p. 25.

58. "Executive Order Implements Civil Justice Reforms," *The Third Branch*, 23 (Nov. 1991): 8.

59. See "Capitol Gridlock," *Newsweek*, Dec. 9, 1991, p. 45; "Nervous and Nasty," *Time*, Dec. 2, 1991, p. 18.

60. Peterson *et al*, *Punitive Damages*, p. 3.

61. See Jolene Limbacher, "Wronged Say Damages Ruling Is a Big Right," *Akron Beacon Journal*, Mar. 15, 1991, p. B3.

62. John A. Stookey, "Does Rodney Dangerfield Deserve Any Respect? Political Science and the Study of Civil Trial Courts," *Law, Courts, and Judicial Process Section Newsletter*, 8 (Fall 1991): 5.

Chapter 9: Judicial Policy-Making: A Concluding Note

1. Harry P. Stumpf, *American Judicial Politics* (New York: Harcourt Brace Jovanovich, 1988), p. 45.

2. William H. Rehnquist, *The Supreme Court: How It Was, How It Is* (New York: William Morrow, 1987), p. 313.

3. Ibid., p. 212.

4. Ibid., pp. 215–34.

5. See Christopher E. Smith, "The Supreme Court's Emerging Majority: Restraining the High Court or Transforming Its Role?," *Akron Law Review*, 24 (1990): 393–421; Christopher E. Smith, "The Supreme Court in Transition: Assessing the Legitimacy of the Leading Legal Institution," *Kentucky Law Journal*, 79 (1990): 317–46.

6. *Wards Cove Packing Co. v. Atonio*, 490 U.S. 642 (1989).

7. *Patterson v. McLean Credit Union*, 491 U.S. 164 (1989).

8. R.A. Zaldiver and Aaron Epstein, "Uncivil Signing: Bush's Rose Garden Ceremony for Rights Bill Spoiled by Leaked Memo on Affirmative Action," *Akron Beacon Journal*, Nov. 22, 1991, p. A1.

9. *City of Richmond v. Croson Co.*, 488 U.S. 469 (1989).

10. See Gerald Rosenberg, *The Hollow Hope: Can Courts Bring About Social Change?* (Chicago: University of Chicago Press, 1991).

11. Ibid., pp. 46–54.

12. Ibid., pp. 107–56.

13. Ibid., pp. 157–69.

14. See Charles A. Johnson and Bradley C. Canon, *Judicial Policies: Implementation and Impact* (Washington, DC: Congressional Quarterly Press, 1984).

15. Rosenberg, *Hollow Hope,* pp. 336–43.

16. Ibid.

17. Ibid., p. 4.

18. See Stumpf, *American Judicial Politics,* pp. 360–61.

SELECT BIBLIOGRAPHY

Alpert, Geoffrey P., Ben M. Crouch, and C. Ronald Huff. "Prison Reform By Judicial Decree: The Unintended Consequences of *Ruiz v. Estelle.*" *The Justice System Journal* 9 (1984): 291–305.

Alumbaugh, Steve and C.K. Rowland. "The Links Between Platform-Based Appointment Criteria and Trial Judges' Abortion Judgments." *Judicature* 74 (1990): 153–62.

Baum, Lawrence. *American Courts: Process and Policy*, 2nd ed. Boston: Houghton Mifflin, 1990.

———. *The Supreme Court*, 3rd ed. Washington, D.C.: Congressional Quarterly Press, 1989.

Binion, Gayle. "The Disadvantaged Before the Burger Court." *Law and Policy Quarterly* 4 (1982): 37–69.

Bork, Robert H. *The Tempting of America: The Political Seduction of Law.* New York: Free Press, 1990.

Camp, William E. and David C. Thompson. "School Finance Litigation: Legal Issues and Politics of Reform." *Journal of Education Finance* 14 (1988): 221–38.

Carp, Robert A. and C.K. Rowland. *Policymaking and Politics in the Federal District Courts.* Knoxville, TN: University of Tennessee Press, 1983.

Chayes, Abram. "The Role of the Judge in Public Law Litigation." *Harvard Law Review* 89 (1976): 1281–1316.

Cooper, Philip J. *Hard Judicial Choices.* New York: Oxford University Press, 1988.

Cox, Archibald. *The Court and the Constitution.* Boston: Houghton Mifflin, 1987.

DiIulio, John J., ed. *Courts, Corrections and the Constitution.* New York: Oxford University Press, 1990.

173

Diver, Colin. "The Judge as Political Pawnbroker: Superintending Structural Changes in the Public Institutions." *Virginia Law Review* 65 (1979): 43–106.

Dolbeare, Kenneth and Phillip E. Hammond. "Inertia in Midway: Supreme Court Decisions and Local Responses." *Journal of Legal Education* 23 (1970): 106–22.

Ekland-Olson, Sheldon. "Crowding, Social Control, and Prison Violence: Evidence from the Post-*Ruiz* Years in Texas." *Law and Society Review* 20 (1986): 389–421.

Epstein, Lee. *Conservatives in Court.* Knoxville, TN: University of Tennessee Press, 1985.

Feeley, Malcolm M. "The Significance of Prison Conditions: Budgets and Regions." *Law and Society Review* 23 (1989): 273–82.

Flicker, Barbara, ed. *Justice and School Systems: The Role of the Courts in Education Litigation.* Philadelphia, PA: Temple University Press, 1990.

Galanter, Marc. "Reading the Landscape of Disputes: What We Know and Don't Know (and Think We Know) About Our Allegedly Contentious and Litigious Society." *U.C.L.A. Law Review* 31 (1983): 4–71.

Gates, John B. and Charles A. Johnson, eds. *The American Courts: A Critical Assessment.* Washington, DC: Congressional Quarterly Press, 1991.

Gibson, James L. "From Simplicity to Complexity: The Development of Theory in the Study of Judicial Behavior." *Political Behavior* 5 (1983): 7–49.

———. "The Role Concept in Judicial Research." *Law and Policy Quarterly* 3 (1981): 291–311.

Glazer, Nathan. "Should Judges Administer Social Services?" *The Public Interest* 50 (1978): 64–80.

Goldman, Sheldon and Thomas Jahnige. *The Federal Courts as a Political System,* 3rd ed. New York: Harper and Row, 1985.

Goldman, Sheldon and Austin Sarat, eds. *American Court Systems.* New York: Longman, 1989.

Graglia, Lino A. *Disaster By Decree.* Ithaca, NY: Cornell University Press, 1976.

Grossman, Joel B. and Austin Sarat. "Access to Justice and the Limits of Law." *Law and Policy Quarterly* 3 (1981): 125–40.

Harriman, Linda and Jeffrey D. Straussman. "Do Judges Determine Budget Decisions? Federal Court Decisions in Prison Reform and State Spending for Corrections?" *Public Administration Review* 43 (1983): 343–51.

Harris, M. Kay and Dudley P. Spiller, Jr. *After Decision: Implementation of Judicial Decrees in Correctional Settings.* Washington, DC: Law Enforcement Assistance Administration, 1977.

Horowitz, Donald. *The Courts and Social Policy.* Washington, DC: Brookings Institution, 1977.

———. "The Courts as the Guardians of the Public Interest." *Public Administration Review* 37 (1977): 148–54.

Howard, J. Woodford. *Courts of Appeals in the Federal Judicial System.* Princeton, NJ: Princeton University Press, 1981.

———. "Role Perceptions and Behavior in Three U.S. Courts of Appeals." *Journal of Politics* 39 (1977): 916–38.

Huber, Peter W. *Liability: The Legal Revolution and Its Consequences.* New York: Basic Books, 1988.

Johnson, Annette B. "State Court Intervention in School Finance Reform." *Cleveland State Law Review* 28 (1979): 325–72.

Johnson, Charles A. and Bradley C. Canon. *Judicial Policies: Implementation and Impact.* Washington, DC: Congressional Quarterly Press, 1984.

Kakalik, James S. and Nicholas M. Pace. *Costs and Compensation Paid in Tort Litigation.* Santa Monica, CA: The RAND Corp., 1986.

Kalodner, Howard I. and James J. Fishman, eds. *Limits of Justice: The Courts' Role in School Desegregation.* Cambridge, MA: Ballinger Publishing, 1978.

Kingdon, John W. *Agenda, Alternatives, and Public Policies.* Boston: Little, Brown, 1984.

Kluger, Richard. *Simple Justice: The History of* Brown v. Board of Education *and Black America's Struggle for Equality.* New York: Random House, 1975.

Macedo, Stephen. *The New Right v. The Constitution.* Washington, DC: The Cato Institute, 1987.

Milner, Neal. "Comparative Analysis of Patterns of Compliance with Supreme Court Decisions." *Law and Society Review* 5 (1970): 119–34.

Morgan, Richard E. *Disabling America: The "Rights Industry" in Our Time.* New York: Basic Books, 1984.

Murphy, Walter F. *The Elements of Judicial Strategy.* Chicago: University of Chicago Press, 1964.

Nieman, Donald G. *Promises to Keep: African-Americans and the Constitutional Order, 1776 to the Present.* New York: Oxford University Press, 1991.

O'Brien, David. *Storm Center: The Supreme Court in American Politics.* New York: W.W. Norton, 1986.

Orfield, Gary. *Must We Bus?: Segregated Schools and National Policy.* Washington, DC: Brookings Institution, 1978.

Peterson, Mark, Syam Sarma, and Michael Shanley. *Punitive Damages: Empirical Findings.* Santa Monica, CA: The RAND Corp., 1987.

Porter, Mary Cornelia and G. Alan Tarr, eds. *State Supreme Courts: Policymakers in the Federal System.* Westport, CT: Greenwood Press, 1982.

Rabkin, Jeremy. *Judicial Compulsions: How Public Law Distorts Public Policy.* New York: Basic Books, 1989.

Rehnquist, William H. *The Supreme Court: How It Was, How It Is.* New York: William Morrow, 1987.

Reid, Traciel V. "Judicial Policy-Making and Implementation: An Empirical Examination." *Western Political Quarterly* 41 (1988): 509–27.

Rosenberg, Gerald N. *The Hollow Hope: Can Courts Bring About Social Change?* Chicago: University of Chicago Press, 1991.

Schwartz, Bernard. *Swann's Way: The School Busing Case and the Supreme Court.* New York: Oxford University Press, 1986.

Schwartz, Herman. *Packing the Courts: The Conservative Campaign to Rewrite the Constitution.* New York: Charles Scribner's Sons, 1988.

Shanley, Michael, and Mark A. Peterson. *Comparative Justice: Civil Jury Verdicts in San Francisco and Cook Counties, 1959–1980.* Santa Monica, CA: The RAND Corp., 1983.

Smith, Christopher E. *Courts and the Poor.* Chicago: Nelson-Hall, 1990.

———. "Federal Judges' Role in Prisoner Litigation: What's Necessary? What's Proper?" *Judicature* 70 (1986): 144–50.

———. "Polarization and Change in the Federal Courts: *En Banc* Decisions in the U.S. Courts of Appeals." *Judicature* 74 (1990): 133–37.

Stumpf, Harry P. *American Judicial Politics.* San Diego, CA: Harcourt Brace Jovanovich, 1988.

Taggart, William A. "Refining the Power of the Federal Judiciary: The Impact of Court-Ordered Prison Reform on State Expenditures for Corrections." *Law and Society* 23 (1989): 241–71.

Tatalovich, Raymond and Byron W. Daynes. *The Politics of Abortion: A Study in Community Conflict in Public Policymaking.* New York: Praeger, 1981.

Tate, C. Neal. "Personal Attribute Models of the Voting Behavior of U.S. Supreme Court Justices: Liberalism in Civil Liberties and Economics Decisions, 1946–1978." *American Political Science Review* 75 (1981): 355–67.

Tate, C. Neal and Roger Handberg. "Time Binding and Theory Building in Personal Attribute Models of Supreme Court Voting Behavior, 1916–1988." *American Journal of Political Science* 35 (1991): 460–80.

Theberge, Leonard, ed. *The Judiciary in a Democratic Society.* Lexington, MA: Lexington Books, 1979.

Thomas, Jim, Devin Keeler, and Kathy Harris. "Issues and Misconceptions in Prisoner Litigation: A Critical View." *Criminology* 24 (1986): 775–97.

Thro, William E. "The Third Wave: The Impact of the Montana, Kentucky, and Texas Decisions on the Future of Public School Finance Reform Litigation." *Journal of Law and Education* 19 (1990): 219–50.

Wasby, Stephen L. "Arrogation of Power or Accountability: Judicial Imperialism Revisited." *Judicature* 65 (1981): 208–19.

———. "Civil Rights Litigation By Organizations: Constraints and Choices." *Judicature* 68 (1985): 337–52.

———. "The Communication of the Supreme Court's Criminal Procedure Decisions: A Preliminary Mapping." *Villanova Law Review* 18 (1973): 1086–1118.

———. *The Supreme Court in the Federal Judicial System,* 3rd ed. Chicago: Nelson-Hall, 1988.

Wolfe, Christopher. *Judicial Activism.* Pacific Grove, CA: Brooks/Cole, 1991.

Yackle, Larry W. *Reform and Regret: The Story of Federal Judicial Intervention in the Alabama Prison System.* New York: Oxford University Press, 1989.

Yarbrough, Tinsley E. "The Alabama Prison Litigation." *The Justice System Journal* 9 (1984): 276–90.

INDEX

177